KT-223-815

Dave Tomlinson is married to Pat and together they have three grown-up children. After twenty-five years of leadership among the house churches, he now convenes an unusual church which meets in a pub in Clapham, South London. Dave has recently taken time out of a busy schedule of itinerant preaching and teaching to complete a Masters degree in Biblical Interpretation. In both his writing and his church involvements, he is particularly concerned to see the gospel made relevant to contemporary culture.

The Post-Evangelical

DAVE TOMLINSON

TRIANGLE

First published in Great Britain in 1995

Triangle
Society for Promoting Christian Knowledge
Holy Trinity Church
Marylebone Road
London NW1 4DU

Third impression 1997

British Library Cataloguing-in-Publication Data
A catalogue record for this book is available from the British
Library

ISBN 0–281–04814–2

Photoset by Dorwyn Ltd, Rowlands Castle, Hants
Printed and bound in Great Britain by BPC Paperbacks Ltd
Member of the British Printing Company Ltd

Dedicated to Steve Fairnie, a true post-evangelical, who left us much too soon.

Contents

1 A Symbol of Hope

It may seem strange to be talking about 'post-evangelical' just as others are talking about an evangelical renaissance, yet the subject is of vital concern to an increasing number of people, who for various reasons, feel the urge to explore new possibilities, with regard to their faith. At the time of writing the term 'post-evangelical' has no formal definition, there is no body of theology behind it, no published agenda and certainly no organization, and yet it is surprising how many people on hearing the word for the first time immediately understand its significance, and have a rough idea what it might imply. Indeed, for lots of them it is a welcome rallying point, a symbol of hope.

Why do people need such a hope, and what do they expect to find? These are the questions we are about to discuss, but first, I should briefly explain a little about this book. Although I talked extensively to many people with different viewpoints, I have not set out to present a survey of their opinions, and I am not writing as a dispassionate onlooker: I consider myself post-evangelical. The book is really intended to operate on three levels. First, it is an apologetic, an explanation of what is going on and why. Second, it is a pastoral response to those who feel confused as to where they stand, and wonder if, perhaps, they are alone in thinking and feeling as they do. I wish to say that probably they are not alone. And third, it aims to discuss some of

the thorny issues and offer possible alternative interpretations to those that such people often feel stuck
with. I believe the lack of ready alternatives is a major
source of people giving up the quest altogether, and
consequently becoming ex-Christians rather than post-
evangelicals.

An example of this is a man I met at a garden party a
couple of years ago. After a brief conversation, he con-
fessed that he had once been an evangelical Christian,
but that he now considered himself an agnostic. On
hearing more of his story, it seemed quite clear to me
that his problems were more to do with the dogmatic
strand of evangelicalism he had encountered than with
God himself. I told him this, and we talked for a long
time about the difficulties which had finally led him to
throw in the towel. He was a thinking person who
could not accept things simply because he was told that
they were so, and unfortunately this is exactly what
had been expected of him. If only there had been space
for him to explore ideas for himself, albeit with guidance and care from others, I believe his story could
have turned out quite differently. Thankfully, he has
now found that space, and is rediscovering a way forward within the Christian faith.

Why 'Post'-Evangelical?

Most of those who contemplate the possibilities of
being 'post'-evangelical do so because of a difficulty
they find in reconciling what they see and experience in
evangelicalism with their personal values, instinctive
reactions and theological reflections. For some people
the agony created by this conflict is very considerable,

as became quite evident in my many conversations with people while I was researching this book. One young man, who had grown up in an evangelical home, spoke with pain about the dilemma: 'I don't know where to go. I no longer feel I can call myself an evangelical, yet I certainly don't wish to be a liberal. What am I?' Other people are more nonchalant about it, like the young woman who told me: 'Evangelicalism helped me to begin with, but I feel I've outgrown it now.' Arrogant? Possibly, yet she was voicing something which cropped up continually in my discussions with people: the feeling that evangelicalism is supremely good at introducing people to faith in Christ, but distinctly unhelpful when it comes to the matter of progressing into a more 'grown up' experience of faith.

What do they mean by 'grown up'? Lots of things, but I will just mention the one which is cited most often: the desire to interact on a more positive level with theologies and perspectives which do not come from an evangelical source.

The feeling people have is that such perspectives are only ever mentioned in evangelical circles in order to be promptly dismissed as rubbish or as a disgraceful compromise. 'I have suffered twenty years of religious and theological censorship', one person exclaimed. 'I have been warned about this and told to keep away from that. I've had enough of it. It's time for me to make up my own mind.' Let me illustrate this point with an analogy. Being a frequent traveller up and down the motorways, I know what it is like to scan the airwaves for something of interest to listen to. I never cease to be amazed at the different ways in which the same news items are reported by various radio stations; sometimes

I wonder if I am hearing about the same events. The contrast becomes even greater if I listen to reports of the same incidents from overseas stations, and if I really want to be confused, I listen to the in-depth commentators, who seem able to produce diametrically opposing views on virtually any subject!

The point is that these people are tired of listening only to the evangelical networks. Indeed, they have already tuned in to other stations and have found that initial confusion has soon given way to great exhilaration, as they realized the diversity of possible interpretations of the Christian faith. A more 'grown up' environment, in their view, would be one in which there were fewer predigested opinions and fewer categorical conclusions, and where there was a lot more space to explore alternative ideas. They would also like room to express doubt, without having someone rush around in a mad panic trying to 'deliver' them from unbelief. Far too often, doubt is portrayed simply as an enemy rather than as a potential friend; as something mature Christians should not suffer from, rather than as a vital means of Christians becoming mature.

The temptation for post-evangelicals is simply to up and leave the evangelical tradition and move elsewhere. For some this may be a good decision, but it would be a great mistake to imagine that the things we are discussing are a mere 'storm in an evangelical tea cup': narrow-mindedness and dogmatism are to be found in churches of all traditions. The theological issues under question may not always be the same, but the feeling of social claustrophobia can be exactly the same, as was demonstrated by a television documentary made by Karen Armstrong, the author and former nun. The similarity between the things Catholics were saying to her about the Roman Catholic Church, and things post-evangelicals might say about evangelical churches, was quite extraordinary. And the same could be said of other traditions: even liberals can be dogmatically liberal! All in all, swapping traditions is not necessarily a solution.

But there is another difficulty about switching churches, because when the chips are down, disillusioned evangelicals quite often discover that their evangelical background still counts for something. At this point, it might be helpful to give a brief explanation of the term 'evangelical'.

What do We Mean by 'Evangelical'?

The evangelical tradition, which incidentally exists across the denominations rather than in any one in particular, has been identified as coming to prominence in at least three periods of Protestant history.[1] Although the term itself derives from the Greek word *euangelion*, meaning 'gospel' or 'good news', its use in this form dates back to the Reformation, when it simply described the emerging Protestant movement, and especially the Lutheran wing of the movement. Then there was the period of the great evangelical revivals during the eighteenth and nineteenth centuries, associated with people like Wesley, Moody and Finney, and lastly, during the late nineteenth and early twentieth centuries, there was the period of evangelical fundamentalism. Each of these periods has contributed substantially to the character of the present-day movement. The Reformation established the supremacy of biblical authority over the authorities of both the Pope and church tradition; it also gave prominence to the doctrine of justification by faith. The emphasis of the evangelical revivals was on personal conversion, holiness of life and the need to preach the gospel. The fundamentalist period was characterized by the defence of the Bible in the face of attacks from science, history and modernist theology.

Although one writer has described no fewer than sixteen distinct strands of evangelicalism,[2] we can, even from this simple historical outline, identify several major features common to all evangelicals. Evangelicals recognize the gospel of salvation through faith in Christ's atoning work as absolutely central; they assert that this faith must be personal, leading to an experience of conversion; they stress the importance of declaring the gospel to those who do not believe, and they hold to the supremacy of Scripture over all other sources of authority. Many argue, like the fundamentalists, for the 'inerrancy' of the Bible (the belief that in its original form it contained no errors or mistakes) and most, in fact, hold a position which is very close to inerrancy, while they may not particularly like the word. It also goes without saying that evangelicals universally believe in the actual historical nature of events like the virgin birth, the miracles, and the death and bodily resurrection of Christ.

It would be quite misleading, however, to describe evangelicalism simply in terms of beliefs: evangelicalism must also be understood in terms of its 'culture', or its social ambience. When a person becomes an evangelical Christian, they are walking into a new world: they will soon discover an entire sub-culture of church services, events, festivals, concerts, conferences, magazines, books, merchandise, record companies, mission organizations, training schemes, holiday clubs and celebrities. They will also encounter distinctive social attitudes and behavioural expectations, which at best might be interpreted as the right way for Christians to live, and at worst are criticized as being christianized, middle-class conservativism. To be fair, there is probably a good mixture of the two.

The upshot of entering this strange new world of evangelicalism is that individuals are expected to change, and they generally do change. How much of this change stems from the Holy Spirit recreating the individual in the image of Christ, and how much is the pressure of a social situation, squeezing that person into the mould of evangelical culture, is a matter of judgment.

What is a 'Post-Evangelical'?

Several people have suggested to me that 'post-evangelical' is really just a fashionable way of saying 'ex-evangelical', but this is not necessarily the case; properly used, 'post' means something quite different from 'ex'. 'Post', which means 'after', has connotations of 'following on from', whereas 'ex' implies 'ceasing to be'. *To be post-evangelical is to take as given many of the assumptions of evangelical faith, while at the same time moving beyond its perceived limitations.* Linguistically, the distinction is similar to the one which sociologists make between the 'modern' and the 'postmodern'. It is taken for granted that in order for something to be postmodern it has to be building on, or be linked with, or be continuous with, that which is modern.

But is 'post-evangelical' still 'evangelical' or is it something quite different? The problem with this sort of discussion is that it becomes horribly theoretical. Who decides where lines are drawn or who is the appointed keeper of the gate of evangelical tradition? Interestingly enough, academics have a similar debate with regard to whether postmodern really is 'post' modern or just another manifestation of modern. Probably the best thing we can do is remind ourselves of the old dictum, that there will be no evangelicals in heaven! No Catholics, no Protestants, no Baptists, Methodists or Orthodox, and no post-evangelicals – just people who love God. Labels may serve some earthly purpose, but in eternal terms they are entirely inconsequential.

A more interesting question concerns the roots and influences of the movement towards being post-evangelical. It is quite clear that personal frustration, hurt and boredom all play their part, but there is much more to it than this. My thesis is that post-evangelicals are influenced by a different culture from the one which helped shape present-day evangelicalism. Sociologists tell us that Western societies have undergone and are undergoing a major cultural shift, from what they call modernity to postmodernity. We will look at the meaning of this more closely in the next chapter. For the time being, we must simply note that during the twentieth century evangelicalism has had to situate itself in the world of modernity, and it has had to experience and express its faith, and contend for the integrity and credibility of that faith, in the cultural environment of modernity. Post-evangelicals, on the other hand, are people who relate more naturally to the world of postmodernity, and consequently this is the cultural environment which influences the way they think about and experience their faith; and this is the context in which the integrity and credibility of their faith must be tested.

Many people will feel distinctly uneasy about such a close connection being made between faith and culture; some may even argue that their faith is based on 'naked' truth, which is unaffected by culture. Nowadays, such a naive view is impossible to sustain; it is now understood that our whole perception of the world – including our faith – is deeply influenced by culture and language. The way we perceive the being and person of God is influenced by culture, the way we think of redemption is influenced by culture, the way we imagine heaven is influenced by culture, the way we approach the Bible is influenced by culture. The idea that we can simply pick up the Bible and read it, devoid of any cultural conditioning is, quite frankly, nonsense: a great gulf lies between the world of the Bible, and our own world. It is a gulf which we can and do seek to bridge both by hard work and by the inspiration of the Spirit, but it is there all the same.

The implications of the cultural differences to which I refer are enormous, and the two most apparent areas which are affected are those of spirituality and theology. It is probably fair to say that the post-evangelical impetus generally begins in individuals, with a growing awareness of surface cultural differences between themselves and their evangelical surroundings: they are irritated by different aspects of evangelical 'culture'. It may be the style of worship, the music, the language, the attitudes towards the rest of the world or the political assumptions. But these things are just the beginnings, and before long differences begin to appear with regard to spirituality and theology.

As we shall see, one of the strands of postmodern culture is a longing for the spirituality which had been squeezed out by materialism and rationalism. In his excellent book *What is the New Age Saying to the Church?*[3] John Drane has shown how and why this spiritual hunger has largely been directed into the New Age movement rather than into the church. The post-evangelical impetus, however, is to search for this fresh sense of spirituality in the symbolic and contemplative traditions of the church rather than in the New Age movement. Failing to find much evidence of these elements in evangelical spirituality, it is inevitable that post-evangelicals seek to find them in ancient Celtic Christianity, as well as in aspects of Catholicism and Eastern Orthodoxy. Post-evangelicals also have a heartening appetite for theology. They not only want to feel the surgings of a fresh spirituality, they want to understand their faith, yet the influence of their culture turns them away from the certainty and absoluteness of much evangelical theology. So where do they turn? This is a key question, and one which we must tackle before we are through.

The only other thing I need to say at this point regarding the nature of the term 'post-evangelical', is that it certainly does not describe a movement as such. John Drane says that it is in the nature of the New Age movement that relatively few people actually label themselves 'New Age', although an enormous number of people identify with some aspects of what New Age stands for.[4] It is fairly similar with post-evangelicalism: very many people who have never even heard of the term 'post-evangelical', much less used it as a self-conscious label, will, I believe, identify strongly with much of what we are discussing. And they may not all be evangelicals.

Footnote: and This is Me

By way of a footnote to this introductory chapter, it may help if I say a few things about myself and the rather unusual church I am involved with, as I shall be making references to it throughout the rest of the book.

My background has been thoroughly evangelical. I grew up in a Brethren Church, and made a personal commitment of faith as a young teenager. Some years later, I received what was called the baptism of the Holy Spirit, and was subsequently asked either to renounce it, or leave the church: this was because the experience of the baptism of the Spirit, which has subsequently become widespread throughout the charismatic movement, was at the time considered by many church leaders as pentecostal 'emotionalism', and something definitely to be avoided. I did leave and became involved in the early house church movement (now generally known as the New Churches). When I reached the tender age of 22, now married to Pat and with a young family, we branched out and planted our first church. This was to open up into twenty years of full-time work among the New Churches, ten years of which were spent leading a team of fifteen people, who gave oversight to some fifty churches.

Toward the end of the 1980s, Pat and I felt we needed a fresh focus in our lives. Without intending to do so, we became caught up with people who were either on the edges of evangelical and charismatic churches or who had fallen off the edge altogether. Much rethinking took place with regard to theological issues and with regard to the way in which churches (of all types and traditions) tend to demand a degree of conformity over and above the essential requirements of the gospel. We were amazed to discover how many ex-churchgoers there were around: people who though they no longer attended church, certainly still retained their faith. Then there were the many people we began to meet at the Greenbelt Arts Festival: people who treated the Festival as their church, but obviously only attended it once a year! I am now convinced that we are aware only of the tip of an enormous iceberg. Literally tens of thousands of people continue to practise their faith privately, whilst finding no real relevance for church in their lives. By no means all of these people are post-evangelical as I am describing it in this book, but if that option had been available to them, I am certain that many of them would still be attending churches.

Believing that Christianity is, in essence, a communal faith, Pat and I and a few other friends began to experiment with a quite different form of church, which might appeal to at least some of these people. The upshot has been a rather unconventional church, facetiously called Holy Joe's, which meets in the lounge bar of a South London pub on Tuesday nights. With its many failings and weaknesses I believe Holy Joe's has demonstrated the possibilities of an alternative church life. Interestingly enough, we have found that it has been a symbol of hope for people in many parts of the country, most of whom have never even attended one of its meetings. How often have I talked with people who have given up on church, who say, 'If only there was something like this where I live.' From time to time we also hear of other similar ventures, in Britain and in other countries, whose inspiration has been drawn from Holy Joe's. And of course, there are many others which have come into being without people ever having heard of Holy Joe's.

The format is simple and the atmosphere very relaxed. People behave as they normally would in a pub: they can drink or smoke, they can participate as much or as little as they wish, and if they really do not like it, they can just move through to the main bar. We have worship evenings, which tend to be quite contemplative, with plenty of candles, symbols, and ambient music, and we have Bible study evenings where people eagerly take part in trying to understand and interpret the Scriptures. Holy Joe's does not set itself up against the traditional churches – several ex-members are now training for ordination in the Church of England – but it is satisfying a need which many churches fail to meet. I am by no means saying that this sort of thing is the way ahead for post-evangelicals; the vast majority will probably (hopefully) remain in their churches, but it is an example of how a group of post-evangelicals are trying to work out their faith communally.

2 *We've Never Had it so Good!*

By any standards, the period from the early 1980s to the mid-1990s has been a remarkable period of transformation for British evangelicalism. In the years prior to this, the expectation of growth in most churches was minimal, media attention was virtually non-existent and the idea of making an impact on society was little more than a pipe-dream. Today, not only has decline in church attendance apparently bottomed out, but many evangelical churches are growing dramatically and new churches are being planted regularly. High profile personalities in politics, entertainment and sport are continually 'coming out' about their faith, and the media pays increasing attention to evangelical and charismatic issues, as demonstrated by the considerable coverage given to the so-called 'Toronto Blessing'. BBC Television's *Songs of Praise* regularly features worship from evangelical and charismatic churches.

Against this very positive background, it is understandable that many would ask why on earth we should be discussing 'post'-evangelicalism. After all, we've never had it so good – at least not in my lifetime. Surely, we should be rejoicing and standing together, and not nit-picking over non-essential differences? Well of course this depends on what is considered non-essential, and the plain fact of the matter is that not everyone feels equally at home with all that is happening; there are questions to be asked. But before saying any more about this, I would like to pinpoint a number of factors which I believe are crucial in the recent change of British evangelical fortunes.

The 'Charismaticizing' of Mainstream Evangelicalism

Initially, during the late 1960s and early 1970s, the renewal movement threatened to split evangelicals irreparably; the terms 'evangelical' and 'charismatic' were almost totally incompatible. To some degree this arose from the fact that many evangelicals reacted violently to renewal, in some cases denouncing it as of the devil. There was also the fact that the renewal cut across the old denominational barriers – even Protestant and Catholic – uniting people with a stronger bond than did identification with evangelicalism. The acrimony and pain created by the early divisions was enormous: even previously close friends and colleagues vilified one another in the name of truth.

By the end of the 1970s, however, much of the heat had gone from the issues; there was calmer dialogue between charistmatic and non-charismatic evangelicals, and more acceptance of one another. Fifteen years later, the situation has changed dramatically: it is now clear that the whole centre ground of evangelicalism has become gradually charismaticized, adopting the style and ethos of the charismatic movement. It is today commonplace in evangelical churches, to find people clapping their hands, waving their arms in the air and singing charismatic choruses; there is even widespread acceptance of gifts of healing and prophecy. And by early 1995, hundreds of evangelical churches had been influenced by the 'Toronto Blessing', which involves people collapsing, laughing uncontrollably and making strange noises, such as barking and roaring. Only a few years ago, this would have been unthinkable.

Overall, charismatic renewal, which initially threatened the unity and well-being of evangelicalism, has actually proved to be a powerful source of its energizing. Of course the appeal is by no means universal: there are still many evangelicals who resist the tide of the charismatic. Yet one cannot help feeling that such resistance is Canute-like.

The Marriage of Mainstream Evangelicalism with the New Churches

A great deal of the animosity between charismatics and evangelicals throughout the late 1960s and 1970s surrounded the emergence of what was then called the house church movement (now known as the New Churches). Although many charismatic leaders consistently opposed the idea of church splits and the setting up of new churches, the development was inevitable, especially since so many of the established churches took such an antagonistic stance towards renewal. Starting from humble beginnings in someone's front room, the small groups were initially written off as a passing fad, but they soon grew and multiplied across the country. Before long, networks developed around strong itinerant leaders, and annual events like the Dales Week and the Downs Week became popular rallying points. The threat posed to evangelical churches grew, as an increasing flow of people left their churches to join up.

Although there was little doubt that the New Churches adhered to fundamental evangelical faith, evangelicalism was seen by them as the embodiment of all that they were leaving behind: narrow-minded legalism, institutionalism and religiosity. In 1975, a book by Gerald Coates and Hugh Thompson, *Not Under Law*,[1] portrayed evangelicalism as modern-day pharisaism, preoccupied with legalistic practices like quiet times and saying grace before meals. Evangelicals, on the other hand, accused New Church leaders of antinomianism (freedom from obligations to the law by virtue of faith), shallowness and complacency about evangelism.

By the mid-1980s, however, everything had changed. As part and parcel of the charismaticizing of evangelicalism the animosity between the New Churches and many evangelicals gave way to positive co-operation. Nowadays, practically all New Churches are paid-up members of the Evangelical Alliance and everyone bends over backwards to defend evangelicalism! This brings us to another important factor in today's situation.

The Emergence of a New Generation of Evangelical Leaders

Neither of the above developments could have taken place without something significant happening at leadership level within evangelicalism – and it did. In the late 1970s and early 1980s a new generation of leaders emerged in the evangelical establishment. In 1983, Clive Calver took responsibility for the Evangelical Alliance; this appointment symbolized powerfully the way that the centre ground of evangelicalism was moving, for Calver is an unashamed charismatic with New Church connections. Unlike many of the New Church leaders at the time, however, he was also very consciously an evangelical, and was eager to see evangelicalism dragged into the late twentieth century. In his book *Marching to the Promised Land* Ian Bradley asserts that it is the energy of Calver, along with his astute utilization of resources such as those from the New Churches, which has been responsible for the revival of the Alliance as a spearhead for the new evangelical movement: 'He transformed what was largely a moribund and backward-looking organisation by replacing traditional evangelicals with younger people from the house church movement, often with charismatic leanings and many drawn from the Mission England Crusade built around Billy Graham's visit in 1984.'[2]

Yet Clive Calver is but the tip of an iceberg: a new generation of leaders has quietly yet effectively taken responsibility in all quarters of the evangelical establishment. On the whole, they are:

- charismatically inclined, if not full-blown charismatics;
- theologically fairly conservative;
- socially and politically aware;
- eager to promote evangelical values within society, as well as the evangelizing of individuals

The achievements of this new generation of evangelical leaders cannot be exaggerated. They have launched massively successful events, multiplied the membership of organizations like the Evangelical Alliance, vastly increased the media profile of the movement, created links with the black-led church community, and gained the first ever licence in the United Kingdom for an official Christian radio station (London Christian Radio, which began broadcasting in 1995).

The Rallying Effect of Large Events

Any movement gains immensely from its ability to gather large numbers, thus giving its followers a sense of strength. During the 1980s and 1990s the evangelical movement has seen this happen in a particularly remarkable way with the emergence of events like Spring Harvest and the March for Jesus. Though they developed quite separately, the combination could not be better: Spring Harvest gathers evangelicals together in huge numbers and provides an effective inspirational platform, whilst the March for Jesus leads them out onto the streets in larger numbers than ever before. The 'feel-good' factor generated by these two events is enormous.

Spring Harvest, which basically takes the form of a massive evangelical family holiday at Butlins with seminars and nightly celebrations, was started in 1979 by Clive Calver and Peter Meadows, the Communications Secretary with the Evangelical Alliance, and gathered a modest 2,700 people. By 1991 it was drawing more than 80,000 people spread around four venues over a period of a month.[3] Apart from building up the spiritual life of the individual, Spring Harvest aims to contextualize evangelical faith socially and culturally and to facilitate the church being 'salt and light' in society. And although it has never been on the public agenda of the event, there is little doubt that Spring Harvest is one of the most influential factors in the charismaticizing of evangelicalism.

Naturally, Spring Harvest has its critics: some people find it too charismatic, others think it is not charismatic enough. Some are disturbed at the evangelical gloss given to its very considerable spread of topics. But despite all this, Spring Harvest undoubtedly meets a massive demand, and it would be difficult to overstate its significance in the present positive climate. People delight in the challenge they receive, in the diversity of subjects covered, and in the spiritual boost provided by the charismatic-style worship, all of which is often lacking back home. 'Don't criticize Spring Harvest', said one satisfied punter, 'until you've been a member of Great Giddifield Methodist Church.'

The *March for Jesus*, was originally organized by the Ichthus Fellowship in 1987 and to their amazement it drew a crowd of 25,000 people keen to declare their faith publicly and pray for the City of London, as they marched along the streets singing and carrying banners. Three years later, there were marches in 600 different towns and cities across the United Kingdom, involving crowds of around 250,000 and in 1994 there were marches taking place worldwide under the banner 'A Day to Change the World', in which an estimated nine million people took part.

At one level the organizers, Gerald Coates, Lynn Green, Roger Forster and Graham Kendrick, declare it to be 'a colourful, carnival-like atmosphere with song, prayer, and a celebration of hope in Christ', but as Ian

Barbour writes, 'there is no doubt that those behind the March for Jesus do see themselves as fighting the forces of evil'; or as Coates succinctly puts it: 'It is our prayer that the tide of evil will be stemmed, darkness will be pushed back and the gospel . . . will run freely throughout our land in the power of the Holy Spirit.'[4] Roger Forster is even more positive; he claims that by marching and worshipping out on the streets, people can 'penetrate the spiritual atmosphere, confuse the enemy and weaken his grip on society', and that the physical, psychological and spiritual forces which stand in the way of the kingdom of God can be driven back.[5]

Such claims raise all kinds of questions which we cannot delve into here. The simple fact is that hundreds of thousands of Christians take to the streets each year. Some of them indeed believe that they are making a significant impact on the spiritual condition of the nation, others simply see it as an opportunity to stand with fellow-Christians in an act of public witness. Again it is quite certain that this event contributes to the overall sense of growing self-confidence among evangelicals.

The Recovery of a Social Emphasis to the Gospel

The evangelicalism which I grew up with was vehemently opposed to what was called 'the social gospel', which of course was associated with liberal theology. The task of Christian mission certainly did not include any sort of social reform; the nearest we ever got to such activity was to send doctors, nurses and teachers into the mission field to work to improve people's lives and then evangelize them.

It was the Festival of Light in the early 1970s which seemed to indicate a change in the wind with regard to social involvement. Thousands of Christians packed Trafalgar Square, and with the help of people like Malcolm Muggeridge and Mary Whitehouse campaigned against moral decline, the increase of pornography, and liberalized laws on homosexuality. Then there were the prolific writings of Francis Schaeffer which also contributed to an awareness of the social implications of Christianity. Almost single-handedly he placed the issue of anti-abortion on the evangelical agenda. John Stott also played a vital part in developing a broader theological framework for mission, incorporating social action alongside evangelism.

But it was during the 1980s that evangelicals really took on board the need for social concern. CARE Campaigns, which emerged out of the old Festival of Light, gave a focus to issues like the preservation of family values, Christian influence in education, medical ethics and the question of abortion. The Evangelical Alliance has also developed a strong voice on social issues; claiming to speak for a million evangelicals, it regularly gains access to the airwaves. Then there is a whole gamut of other evangelical organizations specializing in particular interests: ACET who care for AIDS sufferers, the Jubilee Centre which conducts research on economic and social issues and which launched the 'Keep Sunday Special' campaign, the Christmas Cracker which raises money for the poor of the Third World, and so on. The will on the part of evangelicals to exert influence on society has probably never been stronger. In part this arises out of the increasing level of self-confidence on the part of the movement and in turn it adds greatly to that confidence.

The Shadows of Revival

Revival is a theme embedded in the evangelical psyche, and although most Christians know little of the actual history of revivals, they tend to have in mind images of mass conversions, of people being struck down in the streets as they became conscious of their sins, and of pubs and brothels being forced to close through lack of business. For as long as I can remember, there has been an underlying hope and belief that God will once again visit our land in this way. Yet I cannot recall a period when there was quite such an intensity of emphasis on revival, as there is at present. During the late 1980s, a series of 'prayer meetings' were organized in the National Exhibition Centre in Birmingham under the banner 'Pray for Revival'; probably to everyone's surprise, 12,000 people turned up!

More recent talk of revival, however, has been linked with the 'Toronto Blessing' mentioned earlier in this chapter. Gerald Coates links what is happening to a prophecy given by Peter Obard in a book published in the early 1950s, entitled *From Ploughboy to Pastor*. The prophecy, based on Ezekiel's vision of the dry bones coming to life (Ezekiel 37), stated that a movement of the Spirit was developing in twenty-year cycles. Between 1954 and 1974 the bones would come together; between 1974 and 1994, sinews would be put upon the body (which he interpreted as New Testament churches being planted), and then between 1994 and 2015 God would breathe into the body and the church would become a mighty army.[6] The implication seems to be that what we are seeing now will develop into full revival, and continue for twenty years. Of course, it is recognized that what is presently happening is not revival; it is more modestly declared 'a time of refreshing'. Indeed, Clive Calver warns against seeing the Toronto Blessing as anything other than a beginning: 'I believe that God starts with us,' he says, 'but we don't want it to finish here do we? I like laughing, but I'd like our world to laugh too.'[7]

Since the inception of the charismatic renewal back in the early 1960s there has been a recurring belief that some great move of God is just around the corner. The early Dales Bible Weeks picked up on this, as did John Wimber, with his 'Third Wave'; then there were the 'Kansas Prophets', with Paul Cain's prophecy that revival would break out by the end of 1992. Will this one deliver? Who knows. But as we approach the year 2000, with all its apocalyptic associations, one thing is for sure: anyone talking or writing about revival is likely to get a ready audience and sell books.

So Why Look for an Alternative?

Before moving on, I should just acknowledge two things. The first is that what I have described as the mainstream of evangelicalism might not be thought to be such by everyone. I certainly have not set out to give a survey of the whole of evangelicalism. And second, I do not pretend to have given a comprehensive list of the factors in the recent resurgence of evangelicalism – just a few which have struck me as significant as I have watched (and been involved with) what has taken place over the last twenty-five years. The positive picture I have painted is really intended to underline even more pointedly the question I raised at the beginning: why, in the light of so much progress, are we talking about the 'post'-evangelical?

Ironically, a significant cause of many people's discomfort in the present evangelical scene arises out of the actual climate of success itself. It goes without saying that whenever any group or movement is buoyant and doing well, a dynamic is generated which makes dissent very difficult indeed, and many people feel this. The problem is compounded by things like platform rhetoric, uncompromising stances and the public vilification of alternative points of view. And the charismatic element can add even more pressure, since it often has the underlying suggestion (and sometimes not so underlying) that to resist what is happening is to resist 'what God is doing'. I know for a fact that many people who give the impression of going along with everything that is said and done actually experience all kinds of reservations, which they feel unable to voice or share with others. It is the same old effect of the emperor with no clothes on – nobody dares speak up. If this is to be overcome, leaders have to work very hard at undermining the very dynamic which they are a part of creating, and that can be costly.

Then there is the question of just how deep the changes brought about by the new generation of leaders really go. The style is changed, there is a broadened agenda and a vastly increased public profile; there are hugely successful events and much more of a unified voice, but what lies beneath the surface of the new rejuvenated evangelical movement? Is there a radical rethinking of the evangelical position in the light of cultural and academic developments? Or do we find the same old evangelicalism recycled and re-presented? I would suggest that it is nearer to the latter, and of course there are very many people who will say that this is precisely as it should be. Others would like to see a deeper review of traditional positions: a review which acknowledges more fully that the frame of reference in which evangelical tradition was formed has now changed drastically. The world at the close of the twentieth century is vastly different from that of the late nineteenth and early twentieth centuries, and this has far greater consequences than simply updating our approach and presentation of the gospel: it requires us to rethink the way in which the gospel is perceived.

I have absolutely no doubt that there are significant numbers of people within evangelicalism who share a desire for the movement to undergo just such a radical rethink. I also know that those in positions of influence do not wish this to happen, and I understand why: they do not want anything to split the constituency and thereby undermine its united voice. My severe reservation about this strategy is that it holds the movement back from facing the challenges which it must confront. Lots of us would be in sympathy with evangelicalism if there were more open debate, if instead of being shielded from the disturbing discussions which lie just around the corner, people were facilitated in the task of rethinking and reinterpreting the Christian faith. REFORM, an evangelical Anglican group, are reacting to the new cultural challenge by returning to what many would see as the false certainties of fundamentalism. Others may wish to avoid that course, but it can only be done by facing the pain and uncertainty of a thoroughgoing rethink.

Another issue is the degree to which the rejuvenation of evangelicalism has re-emphasized its own borders. One of the great virtues of the early charismatic movement was its unselfconscious ecumenism. For a while it seemed as though theological and ecclesiastical differences were not the priorities; the focus was on a deeper sense of unity and kinship brought about by the Spirit, and huge psychological barriers and personal prejudices were swept away. Before long there were theological workshops, and the hope was that the whole ecumenical thrust could be recentred and pushed forward by the renewal. Many things have stood in the way of this, and I am personally saddened by the degree to which people rediscovering their evangelical-ness seems to have led to walls being re-built. I do not, for example, recall seeing a Catholic speaker at Spring Harvest. Oh yes, I know that there are all kinds of 'political' problems tied up with anything which appears to be softening the divide between Catholics and Protestants, but it seems to me that in days when terrorists are laying aside their guns and bombs in Ulster, evangelicals should be prepared to upset a few of their own apple-carts.

'Religions in a Confused World'

One last point about the current resurgence of evangelicalism is the possibility of seeing it in the light of a much bigger picture as painted by a French academic Gilles Kepel in his fascinating book *The Revenge of God*.[8] The book is Kepel's account of what he sees as a worldwide resurgence within the three Abrahamic religions of Islam, Christianity and Judaism. Having spent years studying Islam, Kepel became convinced that what he saw taking place within modern Islam was by no means a purely Islamic phenomenon. After careful comparisons he concluded that the resurgences taking place in each of these three faiths (as well as others) have significant sociological connections with each other, and that taken together they reflect powerfully on a shift taking place in the modern world.

According to Kepel the 1970s were crucial, for it was then that the widespread disillusionment with the modern world came to its peak. It was finally clear that rational methods could not resolve the 'messiness' of the human condition and that there was a longing for a more spiritual solution. In his view the process went into reverse somewhere around 1975, when a new religious approach began to take shape, which was aimed no longer at adapting to secular values (as might have been the case with, say the liberal tradition in Christianity), but at recovering a sacred foundation for the organization of society. As Kepel puts it, the aim of Islam was 'no longer to modernize Islam, but to Islamize modernity'. Modernity had failed, and the reason was seen to be a separation from God. In summary, Kepel tells us that this religious resurgence:

- Gains its impetus directly out of the widespread disillusionment with modern, secular values, and their religious counterparts;
- Expresses a longing for a renewed spiritual dimension to life;

- Focuses an aspiration to transform society by re-establishing its spiritual foundations;
- Far from attracting the stereotypical obscurantists, draws in young, educated people (with a marked bias towards the technical disciplines), who are products of the modern world and yet wish to use what that world has given them in order to come against it. They are, typically, disturbed by the fragmentation of society, and are looking for an overarching ideal to which they can be committed.

The strategies for bringing about the transformation of society are twofold: first, 'from above' by using state legislation, and second, 'from below' by evangelizing the masses.

Kepel pinpoints the 1970s as the crucial turning point, in which there was a massive upsurge of spiritual hunger and the beginnings of a desire to influence the shape of secular society. My own comments about British evangelicalism have also emphasized the significance of this period, and for similar reasons: it was the period when charismatic renewal was taking root in the evangelical movement; and it was the period when social reform was restored to the evangelical agenda.

The relevance of Kepel's analysis for our purposes is clear: the resurgence of evangelicalism corresponds closely to a cultural shift, which many people have documented. Of course I would not wish to be reductionist and suggest that everything is accounted for by the cultural or sociological milieu; none of what we have so far discussed is intended to suggest that God is not at work in the changing fortunes of evangelicalism; I am quite sure he is. But an analysis like Kepel's does, however, relativize the more extreme claims of some evangelicals, and it also enables us to examine what is happening from a human perspective, which is very useful.

I would suggest that the cultural shift surfaces within religious communities in two ways. First there is the tendency to seek refuge in the old certainties. At its most extreme, this route is expressed in hard and fast fundamentalism. And second, it surfaces in the tendency to interact positively with the new cultural situation and to reinterpret faith in the light of that cultural situation. This tendency would be seen at the extreme in the theology of Don Cupitt. Most of us are somewhere in between the extremes, yet inevitably we lean more in one direction than the other, and this factor is crucial to our discussion. Later on we will look more deeply at this dividing of the ways, but first, we will think about it on a more practical level.

3 Worlds Apart

As I have already stated, the post-evangelical impetus quite often draws its initial strength from the sense of irritation many people feel with evangelical 'culture'. I would now like to illustrate this with some concrete examples. If it were simply a case of differences of taste over, say, music or films, or style of dress, the problems could doubtless be overcome fairly easily; indeed far greater tolerance exists nowadays with regard to such things. The sort of issues I am talking about are more likely to be thought of by evangelicals as being fundamental to the Christian life, or at least to Christian holiness, hence the problem is rather deeper.

A danger we all face – whatever our background or tradition – is that of absolutizing our own particular notion of what is essential to the Christian faith. Of course this is not simply a modern problem: members of the early church faced it too. Probably the biggest threat to the first-century church came not from outside but from within, in the form of the rift over Judaism. Many of the Jewish Christians argued that the new Gentile believers must submit to Jewish law in order to be real Christians. Paul would have none of it, and the issue had to be cleared up at the Council of Jerusalem (Acts 15.1–29). After great debate a letter was sent to the Gentile believers which stated, 'It seemed good to the Holy Spirit and to us not to burden you with anything beyond the following requirements . . . .' The particular religious and cultural issues under consideration are of little consequence to us today, but the underlying struggle to contextualize and recontextualize the Christian faith in different cultures is of crucial importance.

The setting of mission has repeatedly brought this question to the fore. In the past missionaries went out to foreign fields, and imposed on indigenous peoples a package which incorporated a change of culture as well as a change of heart. Kwame Bediako, a Presbyterian theologian from Ghana, speaks painfully of the way that missionaries wreaked havoc on African culture in the name of the gospel. Their tendency, he says was 'to treat anything pre-Christian in Africa as either harmful or at best valueless, and to consider the African once converted from paganism as a sort of *tabula rasa*, on which a wholly new religious psychology was somehow to be imprinted.'[1] This cultural assumption, Bediako insists, amounted to a 'judaïzing' activity, and a failure to trust converts sufficiently to the Holy Spirit for the moulding of their lives. And quoting an African missiologist, he tells us that the major weakness in the Western missionary movement in Africa lay in the fact that Africa had no Paul![2]

My contention is that middle-class values form the dominant cultural norm in most evangelical churches, and these values function in a similar way that judaïzing did in the early church, by which I mean that they impregnate the very nature of the gospel. The term 'middle class' is now, of course, notoriously difficult to define, since it is widely agreed that the Marxist definition, based on purely economic factors, no longer meets the complexities of the contemporary situation. I think most people use the term to describe an attitude or outlook which is conservative and committed to maintaining traditional ideas about society, family and personal morality. This in itself is no bad thing, representing as it does a perfectly valid point of view. There are two problems about it which I will mention. The first is that it is generally accompanied by an upward materialistic spiral. In his challenging book *A Long Way from Home* Tony Walter says that Christians have tended to move up the social scale and gradually surround themselves with the trappings of a suburban lifestyle. This will often involve periodically moving house into better areas and, as Walter says, the overall effect is to increase the resources of suburban churches at the expense of churches in the poorer areas.[3]

But the more significant problem, from the point of view of our present discussion, is that middle-class evangelicals (and they are not alone in this) create what Walter refers to as 'culture religion', that is, they identify Christianity with the standards, values and attitudes of their own culture: in this case, middle-class culture:

Christians may not be aware of the extent to which they have conformed to a middle-class lifestyle. So many of the public values of society are middle-class that these values, which are far from inevitable or God-given, are taken for granted. Some Christians, because they have one or two taboos such as not drinking or swearing which set them apart from other people, are able to convince themselves that they are not conforming to society. By focussing their attention on gambling or drink, they ignore the

way in which they have unconsciously absorbed
their neighbour's views on virtually everything else.
They strain at a gnat and swallow a whole cultural
mule.[4]

The consequence of confusing Christianity with
middle-class values is that people who do not identify
with that culture reject the church and, in many cases,
the gospel too. And this does not simply affect people
who would call themselves 'working class'; it also affects a whole stratum of people – especially younger
people – who just do not identify with the status quo of
the establishment at all. One such person told me: 'To
be quite honest, there isn't much apart from faith in
Jesus that I share in common with these people; but the
frightening thing is that they seem to feel sure I will
"improve" and become like them, given a bit of time
and some working on by the Holy Spirit. I doubt if I
will stay around that long.'

Many examples could be given of ways in which
middle-class values and Christian standards are mud-
dled together. We will look at just two broad areas.

The Normative Nature of the Traditional Nuclear Family

Evangelicals join many other conservative sections of
the church in seeing the preservation of traditional
family values as a primary social cause, and I have no
doubt that post-evangelicals share some of their concerns. Few other subjects, however, bring to the surface the differences between traditional evangelicals
and post-evangelicals quite so effectively as the family.

The big question is, what do we mean by family values? In my view, what is meant by values is not really values at all: it is a particular model of family which is being singled out and placed on a pedestal. In this ideal form I doubt if such families exist, or have ever existed, yet the model retains a kind of sacred status.

From a middle-class evangelical perspective, family values means first and foremost the *sanctity of marriage*, that is, the lifelong commitment of one man and one woman within a legally recognized marriage. Christians of all persuasions will probably agree on the desirability of lifelong, faithful partnerships, though there may be less agreement on whether this must take place in the context of a formal marriage. The reason for this reservation is obvious: on average half the couples currently getting married in England and Wales have lived together first. From an evangelical point of view such an arrangement is almost invariably unacceptable, since couples who simply live together are not really counted as married and are consequently 'living in sin' (though the phrase is somewhat out of vogue). Many post-evangelicals see this as ridiculous, especially since there are plenty of couples co-habiting, many of them Christians, who are quite evidently as committed to their relationship as any formally married couple, in many cases more so. The desirability of a formal partnership is not necessarily in question; the issue is the inflexibility of those who are unwilling to accept the validity of marriage when it exists in essence.

Without delving too far into the theology and history of marriage, there are a couple of points worth noting. First, there is surely a substantial difference between a casual relationship in which people live together and a committed relationship. As Anne Borrowdale points out, 'A cohabiting couple who are committed to an exclusive, permanent, faithful relationship are often said to be fulfilling the conditions of marriage, even though they have not gone through a ceremony.'[5] And conversely the presence of a wedding certificate in no way guarantees such a relationship. As Karl Barth once said, 'Two people may be formally married and fail to live a life which can seriously be regarded as married life. And it may happen that two people are not married and yet, in their precarious way, live under the law of marriage.' A wedding, he continues, 'is only the regulative confirmation and legitimation of a marriage before and by society. It does not constitute marriage.'[6] Adrian Thatcher makes a similar point: 'The ceremony is the means of public recognition of a marriage relationship that already exists.' Thatcher acknowledges that such a train of thought is disconcerting for the church, but says that we must accept that marriages do not necessarily have tidy beginnings, and that the ceremony is an event within the history of a couple growing into marriage, rather than the event which creates marriage.[7] The actual way in which people 'get married' in our society is after all a cultural practice which has evolved over centuries.

It is true that couples who get married after cohabitation are more likely to divorce, although the reasons for this are by no means as straightforward as many traditionalists would like to believe. The fact of the matter is that the practice of marriage is evolving in our society, and it is clear that whether people have or have not cohabited prior to a formal marriage does not guarantee a successful future for a relationship. I am not advocating a laissez faire response, which simply goes with the flow; I believe Christians still have an enormous amount to contribute to the present situation, but we cannot do it from a place of rigid traditionalism.

Another important aspect of family values is that of proper *roles and responsibilities*. The accepted traditional roles within the family are well understood: the husband is the head and therefore the final authority; as the main breadwinner he is also responsible for providing for his family, and he is responsible for the behaviour and discipline of the children. The wife's place is to support her husband and wherever necessary to submit to him; she is the home-maker, with the responsibility of caring for domestic affairs and looking after the children. The role of both parents is to ensure a loving and disciplined atmosphere for their children.

Present-day evangelical attitudes are on the move so far as this traditional format is concerned. They recognize that many women need or choose to go out to work, and this is acceptable provided the children and home do not suffer. Marriage is now seen much more as a partnership with decisions being shared, even though the 'headship' of the man generally remains. But post-evangelicals, for the most part, are heirs to a completely different, post-feminist culture. They assume sexual equality and take for granted the right of a woman to follow a career. They have no reservations about house-husbands, if that is what both partners agree, and they see no reason why men should be in charge; roles are a matter of arrangement.

There can be little doubt that evangelicals also see family as being a *two-parent* affair. There may be great sympathy with, and indeed support for, single parents, but the 'ideal' is clear and felt to be clear by those who are single parents. I know several single mothers who have left churches, tired of being patronized or of being made to feel that theirs are second-class families. Some have even been offered substitute fatherly input for the children: 'They always seem to assume that I can't do as good a job', one angry mum said, 'and yet I think I'm doing better than most of them.'

Lastly we should perhaps mention the most basic assumption of all: that getting married or having a partner and subsequently having children is the norm. I am quite sure that many church leaders will deny that such an assumption exists, but years of listening to single people has convinced me that it does. Anecdotes abound of people being asked when they are going to get married, or when they are going to have children. The most blatant example of this came from a woman in her mid-thirties with a reputation for being a 'women's libber'. When she told a group of (male) church leaders that she had no plans to get married, she was actually asked if she was a lesbian. When she replied (rather graciously, I think) that she was not, they said, 'Oh, so you *will* get married if the Lord gives you a husband then?' Although this is an extreme instance of such prejudice, the underlying assumptions are far from exceptional, and they are embedded in the way most churches function. For example, there is the constant and widespread use of the term 'family church'. This may be a positive selling point for families, but it is quite the opposite for many unmarried people. Even more significantly, there is the plain fact that leadership is almost exclusively exercised by married people (usually men). These things speak much louder than words.

Is there common ground on family values between evangelicals and post-evangelicals? Most certainly. Both would no doubt agree on the importance of *love, commitment, faithfulness* and *responsibility* as fundamental biblical principles and requirements. What we need more agreement on is that the values themselves are what really count, rather than the particular forms in which they are expressed. Families and family life are of crucial importance to us all, but as Tony Walter says, the healthy future of the family will be ensured not through absolutizing or idolizing it, but by putting it under scrutiny and by providing a critique of it.[8]

There are many other aspects to this subject, not least the matter of gay partnerships. From a conservative point of view, few things evoke such violent reactions as the suggestion that gay couples might legitimately live together within the same parameters as heterosexual couples or, even worse, act as parents. Unfortunately, if I were to do any justice to such a vast and emotive subject, I would need to abandon my intentions for the rest of this book, so I will have to leave it for another day.

The Confusion of Holiness with Respectability

'Joining the church is like joining a very exclusive club.' I well remember the discomfort this statement brought me. It came from a man who had experienced a dramatic conversion to Christ from a life of heavy drinking, wife-beating and petty crime. He was entirely uncultured so far as Christian behaviour was concerned, but the middle-class folk in the church I pastored were delighted to have such a 'good catch'. They could put up with the 'inconsistencies' and the lapses into old behaviour – for a while. But after a couple of months they were thinking that he needed some 'deeper work of God'. They liked the fact that he had such a nasty past, just so long as in the present he was becoming more like them. It was around this time that he made the statement about the church being like a club; it was a club in which he felt he could never be a full member.

It all came to a head one evening when three respected church members confronted me; they thought that I should put pressure on him to fit in and stop being so awkward, to 'let the Lord have full control of his life'. I refused, saying that perhaps it was we, who needed to listen to him. Then followed the ultimatum: 'Either he goes, or we do.' God knows, I needed their money, but I have never been very good with ultimatums. They left and he stayed! He certainly continued to grow in his faith, but he never did fit into the mould of the respectable Christian. Years later we have Holy Joe's, a church in a pub which has turned out to be a place of refuge for people like him: people who do not fit into the mould and yet who love God and want to pursue their faith in an alternative way.

This man is far from alone in feeling that the church is a kind of exclusive, middle-class club. Many people continually struggle with the expectations they find laid on them to change their behaviour and fit in. Any ongoing group, Christian or otherwise, will have its accepted behavioural norms and its taboos. The problem with churches is that they so often equate their group norm with required Christian behaviour. As we saw at the beginning of the chapter, this is not a new problem in the church: taboos have existed since its inception. In more recent times, people like Moody condemned the perceived sins of the nineteenth century. What he described as 'the four great temptations that threaten us today' were the theatre, disregard for the Sabbath, Sunday newspapers and atheistic teachings, including evolution.[9] All of these were still taboos in my early childhood in the Plymouth Brethren, along with going to the cinema, smoking, drinking, gambling and even attending football matches – quite a burden to carry for a keen Liverpool supporter!

Nowadays, the ground has moved rather, and some of these practices have become legitimate, whilst others still remain off-limits. If in doubt, study the following:

HELPFUL UP-TO-DATE GUIDE TO CHRISTIAN
BEHAVIOUR

Smoking:	No – not really.	Some do in private (especially cigars).
Drinking	OK.	Not generally in pubs, except nice country ones.
Theatre/ cinema:	OK – yes.	Provided it's wholesome.
Gambling:	No.	Apart from the stock exchange.
Sunday papers:	OK.	Provided they're the broadsheets.

Horoscopes:	No.	Some do have a sneaky look.
Pre-marital sex:	No.	Never admit to it in public anyway.
Swearing:	No – not really.	Definitely not in public.

Facetious? Yes, but no less accurate for being so.

Another example of taboo in most evangelical churches, which I have not mentioned in that list, is that of 'smutty' humour and innuendo. For some reason or other there are very few aspects of sex which we are allowed to laugh about. The reasons for this seem to fall onto one or other side of a great divide: sex is thought of either as a 'vulgar' subject, which only vulgar people make jokes about, or as a 'sacred' subject, which we dare not make jokes about. This highlights an interesting ambivalence towards sex, which betrays the fact that middle-class evangelicals have never sorted out how to deal with it in a relaxed way. If it were just a matter of whether or not we laugh at particular jokes, it would not be so bad, but unfortunately this awkwardness about the subject seeps out into much more serious areas, and, consequently, things which need to be talked about openly and candidly are all too often left in the shady fringes. C.S. Lewis offers a much more healthy attitude to sexual humour. He says that it is no coincidence that every language and literature in the world is full of jokes about sex. 'Many of them may be dull or disgusting', he says, 'and nearly all of them are old.' But he insists that they all embody an attitude towards sexuality which endangers the Christian far less than a reverential gravity. Indeed, he warns that we cannot treat the subject entirely seriously without doing violence to our humanity.[10]

It is normally not difficult to detect those who visit Holy Joe's from other churches; they give the impression of being ill at ease in a pub environment. As they look around at the apparent incongruity of people sitting in a pub, perhaps smoking, probably drinking, and yet talking, at times passionately, about God, Christianity and the world in general, they invariably ask me the question: what's the difference between you and the rest of the world? It is an interesting question and, I suspect, slightly reminiscent of conversations between Jesus and the Pharisees – 'there is a glutton and a drunkard, a friend of tax collectors and sinners' (Luke 7.34). The real issue is: in what ways are we supposed to be different from the rest of the world? We must return again and again to the wise conclusion of the early apostles: that believers should not be saddled with greater burdens than is absolutely necessary. Rather than perpetuating religious taboos, we need to decide what is really necessary and then leave the rest for people to decide for themselves. Tony Campolo reminds us of our true priorities:

Both U.S. and U.K. evangelicalism have defined a Christian as someone more pious than the rest of the world. Personally, piety turns me off! The Christian is radically compassionate, not pious. What did people say about Jesus? They didn't call him pious! He had a lousy testimony. Did anybody ever call him spiritual? They called him winebibber, glutton, someone who hangs around with whores and publicans. Jesus was too busy expressing compassion to measure up to the expectations of piety. And I think we need to be more Christ-like.[11]

Without doubt, there are those in evangelical (and other) churches who want a ready-made, pre-packed Christian morality, who do not want the headache of having to think through difficult issues for themselves. Yet there are many others who are tired of being told what is right and what is wrong. Their desire is to grow up in their faith, and they believe that the only way to do this is by taking full responsibility for their thoughts, decisions and actions. Sadly they often find the evangelical environment unconducive to such growth. We need to ask why.

4 Longing to Grow

I want to tell you a couple of stories. The first is about Barbara who was a 'mish-kid' (child of missionaries). Although she had always been included in the church family with her folks, she had been taught from quite an early age that she would need to come to a faith of her own. After going through university where she had had plenty of opportunity to develop her independence and think about life for herself, she decided at 22 to make an open profession of faith in Christ at an evangelistic meeting she attended. Delighted and exhilarated she went along to a local evangelical church. It took around three months for her misgivings to crystallize: 'They just seemed so content with a faith that asked no questions', she told me. 'Everyone calmly accepted whatever the leaders said.'

She moved on and tried several similar churches, but always came to the same point of disillusionment. 'They appeared threatened by the level of my questioning', she continued, 'and told me that I needed to let my doubts go and trust the Lord.' Eventually Barbara faced the choice either to lay aside her questions and stick with this kind of church, or go with her questions and look elsewhere. She chose the latter, eventually joining a liberal Anglo-Catholic church. Thriving in her faith – questions and all – she says that she will always be grateful for what evangelicals gave her, but regrets that they could not take her any further.

The next story has not ended quite so well – yet! James was the minister of a thriving charismatic church. After years of burying his intellectual problems about Christianity under a sea of pastoral work and Sunday sermons, he suddenly hit a major inner crisis which he could not shrug off. I spent several hours walking round the local park listening to an endless stream of doubts and confusion. I told him that I shared many of his questions, and assured him that the pressure would diminish if he would admit to them more openly rather than burying them under his professionalism. Unfortunately he felt that his situation was not that simple. 'When I hinted to my deacons about what I was feeling, they practically had kittens', he said. 'They told me that I was employed to build people's faith up, not to undermine it.' Sadly, he has now left the church altogether and makes no profession of faith – but who knows?

These two post-evangelical accounts are not untypical; most evangelical churches experience a through-flow of people who at some point have been profoundly helped by their evangelical encounter only to become disillusioned further down the road. I myself know hundreds of people who have either moved to non-evangelical churches or who no longer attend any church at all. Why does this happen to some people while others apparently remain perfectly happy? No doubt there are many explanations. In this chapter, however, we shall explore the question with the help of two psychological models.

Stages of Personal Growth

It is now well understood that people pass through different stages in their personal development, and these stages have been analysed in different ways.[1] I have chosen a fairly straightforward example which seems to have a lot of common-sense behind it: that of Scott Peck's four stages of spiritual growth, discussed in his book *The Different Drum*.[2]

In his psychotherapy practice Peck noticed an interesting phenomenon: that religious people who came to him in pain and trouble frequently left the therapeutic process as atheists, agnostics or at least sceptics. On the other hand, atheists, agnostics and sceptics often left therapy as deeply religious people. Same therapy, same therapist, and each of the cases successful in their own terms, and yet with utterly different outcomes from a religious perspective. After puzzling over this for some time, he concluded that the different reactions were connected to the different stages of personal development in each patient undergoing therapy. He also concluded that these stages of personal development, which are common to us all, form an identifiable pattern of progress throughout our lives. It follows from this that just as it is a positive thing for some patients to adopt religious faith, so it is equally positive for others to reject it. Why? Because their faith is more an expression of conformity than a fully independent choice. Hopefully they will rediscover their faith at a later point, but this time as a more enlightened decision. Not that the earlier experience would be invalid; it would have been a genuine expression of what the person felt at the time.

Like any model Peck's is an over-simplification, and most people fit somewhere between the stages. I have changed some of his wording slightly, since I find his rather ambiguous:

STAGE I: Self-obsessed
STAGE II: Conformist
STAGE III: Individualist
STAGE IV: Integrated

Stage I is the normal state of most children, though Peck reckons that around 20 per cent of all adults are also still at this stage. When the shift from Stage I to Stage II occurs in adult life, it often appears sudden and dramatic. It might well be linked to a religious conversion, but it could equally happen through another experience which creates a sudden shift of attitude, like getting married or having a child, or through a close encounter with death, or deciding to resolve a drink problem by joining Alcoholics Anonymous, or whatever. Many dramatic conversions to Christianity take place in people who need a shift from Stage I to Stage II. Others of us who, for example, are already in Stage II before becoming Christians, will probably have a much less dramatic experience – and consequently feel inferior, because we interpret the drama of another person's experience as a sign of greater divine power at work in them.

Peck maintains that most believers and churchgoers are in Stage II of their development, which he calls 'formal', since they become attached to the forms (as opposed to the essence) of their religion. They will vigorously oppose any attacks on, or attempts to change, its canons, liturgies or traditions, which they accept virtually uncritically. Stage II people almost inevitably prefer to see God as transcendent and struggle with notions of immanency; despite their belief that God is loving, their strongest image is of a God of judgment. Peck says that 'it is no accident that their vision of God is that of a giant benevolent Cop in the Sky, because that is precisely the kind of God they need – just as they need a legalistic religion for their governance.'

Despite the fact that Stage III people are frequently non-believers, 'they are generally more spiritually developed than many content to remain in Stage II.' Stage III, which Peck calls the sceptic stage, is certainly all about doubting and questioning; everything which has been taken for granted crumbles, and standard explanations just will not do. At worst, people in Stage III are downright cynical, which creates havoc for Stage II friends who cannot understand the apparent reverse-conversion back to unbelief. But the agnosticism fades as Stage III wears on and affirmations of faith begin to reappear, though not with the naivety of previous stages.

I have called Stage IV 'integrated' since this is the stage when things really come together, not with the simplistic certainty of Stage II but with a more intuitive sense of wholeness or inter-connectedness. Peck calls this the mystic-communal stage, because the drive for objective understanding has moderated under the sense of what cannot be fully grasped and yet is still to be sought after.

There are several important points about this matrix:

- The stages are *only milestones*, and there are multiple gradations within and between them.

- We all regress through earlier stages of our development in certain situations.
- The model is not pejorative. It *describes* stages we all pass through and, to some extent, continue to pass through. There is no 'right' or 'wrong' about being in a particular stage.
- People become Christians at each of the levels and this inevitably has a bearing on the kind of conversion they experience, as well as on the perspective they have on the Christian life and faith in general.

Peck comments that Stage IV men and women will frequently enter religion through an attraction to mystery, whereas Stage II people enter religion to find concrete answers. When we discussed Peck's model at Holy Joe's, one man was brave enough to admit that he wanted a more conformist experience of Christianity and that he struggled when faced with too much uncertainty and ambiguity. Thankfully, the group resisted any temptation to argue him into a different position, and simply reassured him that his feelings were perfectly valid.

I think, in a very approximate way, a lot of post-evangelicals are people who are moving from Stage II to Stage III. This does not make them any more intelligent or clever than those who remain contentedly in Stage II, and their next steps can be varied, as our two opening stories show. Incidentally, some people who appear to be post-evangelical are actually regressing to Stage I and, not to put too fine a point on it, might be better described as pre-evangelical.

The more important question is why so many folk who progress to Stage III or IV feel the need to move on from evangelicalism to some other expression of the church, or to abandon formal churchgoing altogether. It seems as though the sociological (to say nothing of the theological and spiritual) environment of evangelicalism does not accommodate people at these stages as effectively and easily as it does those at Stage II. Perhaps this is because of the definitiveness of evangelical faith, with respect to both its theology and morality. An environment which can comfortably accommodate Stage III people, for example, has to be much freer with its definitions and expectations, and to the average evangelical that smacks of liberalism!

There is another point, however, which Peck does not explore, but which undoubtedly complicates this process even more. It is the way in which people who are otherwise in Stage III or IV seem to regress to Stage II when it comes to the religious part of their lives. Peck's model, which concentrates on a straightforward progression through the stages, is not geared to deal with this phenomenon, so for this we shall now turn to a different model which specifically deals with the way that we switch from one pattern of behaviour to another, depending on the situation.

Childsplay

Transactional analysis, which was originated by Eric Berne and set out in his book *Games People Play*,[3] is based on the recognition that we are multiple natured beings, and that in the course of life different modes or patterns of behaviour are activated, so that certain people or situations bring out one form of response from us, while other situations or people evoke something quite different. The switch of behaviour pattern can be quite stark, and even visibly recognizable, through body language, gestures and words. Transactional analysis specifies three basic modes of behaviour: Parent, Adult and Child. I should say that these terms do not refer to the literal designations of parent, adult or child, but to emotional responses. Because they are being used in this technical sense the words are capitalized, to avoid confusion with more common usages.

Regardless of our age, most of us know what it is like to have a compliant Child reaction when we meet authority figures like policemen, teachers or even parents. It can suddenly and irrationally emerge, even though we know that such a response is no longer necessary. The Parent mode of behaviour, expresses itself through superiority or criticism and majors on 'shoulds' and 'oughts' and verbal put downs. The Adult pattern of behaviour emerges when we feel accepted on equal terms, or when we feel respected and listened to. Each of these behaviour patterns is triggered, according to Berne, by mental and emotional recordings from earlier experiences being played back subconsciously.

In his book *I'm OK – You're OK*, Thomas Harris demonstrates the way people shift behaviour patterns by giving the example of a thirty-four year old woman who came to him with a problem of sleeplessness and worry about 'what I am doing to my children'. During the first part of a one-hour session she wept and said, 'You make me feel like I'm a three-year old.' When asked why she felt this way she said, 'I don't know. I suddenly felt like a failure.' At a later point, when talking about her children, her manner and voice changed dramatically. She became critical and dogmatic: 'After all, parents have rights too. Children need to be shown their place.' During this one-hour session the woman displayed three distinct personalities: one of the reasoning, logical grown-up woman who first entered the surgery; one of the small child dominated by feelings; and one of a self-righteous parent.[4]

The Child pattern has several variations, but for this purpose we shall concentrate on what is called the compliant Child. I find it remarkable that so many evangelicals relate to God and their Christian faith in this compliant Child mode. What is even more remarkable is the number of such people who have extremely well developed Adult modes of behaviour in other areas of their lives. A friend recently spoke with despair of the way in which doctors, lawyers and business people in his church seem to settle for an incredibly simplistic version of faith, despite their training and professional responsibilities. It is as if they walk into church, switch off their critical faculties, and proceed to go along with virtually all that is said and done. It is easy to see how this happens when people are first converted: the experience is surrounded by imagery of new birth and childhood, and the new convert has a strong sense of being a novice with regard to Christianity. The dilemma is that so many of these people appear to get stuck at this stage rather than progressing to a more mature level.

It should also be said that the problem is not limited to the intellectual dimension; a disturbing number of evangelicals appear neurotic and suffer from poor self-image. How many times does one hear people (even from the pulpit) explaining quite small details of their lives in terms of God or the devil. If anything good happens it is the Lord: 'The Lord helped me find this job' or 'God showed me what I should do', whereas bad things are either of the devil or traced back to failure on the part of the individual: 'The enemy was really having a go at me' or 'I should have been obedient to the Spirit.'

All of these reactions, whether of uncritical compliance or neurotic reasoning, are classic Child mode responses, and the paternal Parent voice can be heard quite clearly in the background: 'You mustn't question what God says', or 'If you believe that, you'll go off the tracks', or 'You must be obedient to God's word', or 'If you obey God, everything will work out right.' I have to say that I have frequently returned from preaching trips and turned in desperation to non-believing friends for a bit of sanity.

Parental pressure

The reason for many people dropping out of evangelical churches is their dislike of the Parentalism which dictates exactly what they should believe and how they should behave. In some cases the 'shoulds' and 'oughts' come across very blatantly and, for example, church membership might hinge on the acceptance of prescribed doctrines or codes of behaviour. In other cases the pressure to conform may be more subtle, and suggestive – yet no less powerful for that.

On the doctrinal front you can tell when you are in evangelical territory when you hear the phrase 'Bible-believing'. It is a phrase you constantly come across in the evangelical press or at events like Spring Harvest. But what lies behind it? As John Barton points out, most non-conservative, non-evangelical Christians do in fact honour and value the Bible as well,[5] so why do evangelicals lay claim to this title? The answer of course stems from its historical conflict with liberalism, which has shaped and influenced the character of evangelicalism to a massive degree. A fear of theological woolliness has generated a near obsession with doctrinal correctness. Numerous churches and events will not allow speakers on the platform or in the pulpit unless they openly subscribe to an evangelical statement of faith, and many have not been invited back because they failed to adhere entirely to its every point. Such a Parental policy fails to acknowledge that people who arrive at very different conclusions may nonetheless have done their theology with great integrity and be just as fervent for the truth (and be well worth listening to), and that evangelical believers do not need to be protected in a disinfected bubble of evangelical purity – they can only benefit from exposure to other points of view and consequently from having to make up their own minds.

And fear of the 'slippery slopes' of liberalism does not stop with a concern for doctrinal purity; the 'shoulds' and 'oughts' of the Parent are equally rampant in the area of Christian behaviour. Between the liberals undermining biblical standards and the secularists saying that anything goes, it is felt imperative to leave people in no doubt as to what is expected. Now I appreciate that young people need guidance, but there comes a point at which everyone must be allowed to make their own choices – even if they are wrong ones!

One young unmarried couple who were asked if they were sleeping together reacted on behalf of many others by asking, 'What has that got to do with you? We are living our own lives before God, and we're happy to take responsibility for our actions. Why should we tell you whether we are sleeping together or not?' (As it happens, they were not.) Evangelical culture is laden with taboos, many of which owe more to middle-class respectability than to real holiness, and which all too often only pressure people into living dual lives.

The dominant style of leadership in evangelical churches is Parental. In the name of no-nonsense, no compromising, 'give it to 'em straight' preaching of righteousness we have a classic enactment of the paternal Parent, with an inevitable response of compliance or rebellion. 'That's right', I hear someone say, 'bring them to the point of decision.' But is it the right decision? The only decision which really counts is that which arises out of genuine conviction, not coercion or the pressure of group dynamics. The apostle Paul speaks of sin reviving when the law comes, and he goes on to show that the law was powerless to effect real change (Romans 7 and 8). A lot could be learned from modern management and teaching techniques, in which old-style directional leadership has given way to an emphasis on facilitating people learning for themselves, and making fully independent decisions – a much more Adult and, I believe, spiritual approach.

The Awakening Adult

As post-evangelicals endeavour to move forward from a compliant Child mode, they must take care that they do not simply switch to a rebellious Child mode, which is the flip side of compliance. Both compliance and rebellion are basically defences against the imposition of authority, and they are equally ineffective in terms of making any progress. Paul's comments in Romans 7 indicate that rebellion is actually as much a manifestation of being under the law as is the vain attempt to comply with its demands. What he speaks of in Romans 8 as being 'in Christ' is a position of faith which supersedes both rebellion and compliance.

Transactional analysts speak of a Child mode called 'The Little Professor', or the awakening adult, which is a very helpful concept for our present reflections, since it offers a constructive way forward. The Little Professor is a state characterized by experimentation, inquisitiveness, creativity and constant questioning, which sounds a pretty fair description of where a lot of people find themselves in respect to their faith. Moving out of what my business consultant friend described as 'one of the most stifling environments for creativity that I've ever known', post-evangelicals have a longing to explore their faith without being surrounded by 'No Admittance' signs. A young man, who had grown up in an evangelical family, spoke of the enormous relief he had found in attending a post-evangelical group, where he had been able to explore openly questions which he said would have 'completely freaked' his parents. 'It's like the freedom I felt when I took my "L" plates off my car', he said, 'and I suddenly realized I could go wherever I wanted.' It is a feeling which is both exhilarating and scary.

St Paul's comments about being renewed in the mind might offer some unexpected encouragement. All too often this idea is considered from a purely negative perspective: the kind of thoughts we should not be thinking. This is typical of the way that pietistic Parentalism always defines what we are supposed to be by what we are not supposed to be; hence the new way of thinking is not to think in the old way of thinking. Of course we can take it as read that a renewed mind is a mind being released from the paralysis of greed, lust and selfishness, but I think it also means being freed from narrowness, prejudice and complacency, so that we can proceed to explore with freedom and imagination.

I shall close this chapter by simply listing some of the qualities we might expect to find in a mind which is being renewed. First we might expect it to be an *open* mind, which is honest and willing to reconsider its position continually. By open I do not mean gullible – quite the reverse; an *open* mind thrives on doubts and questions but is not ultimately governed by them. It is always prepared to listen, even to the most outlandish ideas, and to consider that there may be things which can be learned from what is being said.

Second, we might expect it to be open to *creative* and *lateral* possibilities. Edward de Bono, who popularized the term 'lateral thinking', has shown us the way in which so much thinking is locked into straight furrows and mental ruts. Lateral thinking is when we break out of these furrows and consider unusual, maybe obscure, connections between different ideas. It means putting together thoughts or concepts which have previously been considered incompatible. In these days of academic inter-discipline and religious ecumenism the possibilities are endless. I have now given up worrying when people tell me, in Parent mode, 'you can't do that' or 'you'll end up with a mixture'; evangelicals have made a god out of doctrinal and religious purity. Humility alone should tell us that we can learn from others.

A third expectation we might have of a renewed mind, is that it should be *reflective*, rather than merely accumulating information. Harry Blamires makes a similar differentiation between scholars and thinkers (forgive his sexist language): 'Potential thinkers are being turned into mere scholars . . . . The thinker challenges current prejudices. He disturbs the complacent. He obstructs the busy pragmatists. He questions the very foundations of all around him, and in so doing throws doubts upon aims, motives, and purposes which those running affairs have neither time nor patience to investigate. The thinker is a nuisance.'[6] I disagree that scholars are necessarily accumulators rather than thinkers (a point he moderates later on), but Blamires expresses perfectly the quality of reflective thinking which I espouse as being characteristic of the renewed mind.

One other element we might expect of the renewed mind is that it be *holistic*, by which I mean that it incorporates emotion, intuition and mystery as equal partners with rationality. Critical reason alone produces a false consciousness which is inevitably reductionistic. As we shall see, this is an important area of divergence between post-evangelicals and liberals, whose reliance on reason discounts cognitive contributions from the non-rational.

5 Woolly Liberals?

And so to the crunch question: isn't post-evangelical just another way of saying 'woolly liberal'? It never ceases to amaze me how paranoid evangelicals are about liberalism. Any deviation from the 'straight and narrow' and, 'Whoa! I think you need to be careful there, you're sounding like a liberal.' 'Liberal' is of course a wonderful blanket term, which describes almost anything that deviates from the accepted evangelical line on things. It is my contention that 'post-evangelical' does certainly not mean 'liberal', and I would deeply regret it if, out of a lack of viable alternatives, post-evangelicals drifted towards liberalism, though I probably feel this for different reasons from those that many evangelicals would put forward.

'The Bogey-Man Will Get You!'

We are all familiar with the silly tactic used by some parents of threatening their children with the bogey-man: 'If you go out there, the bogey-man will get you.' It is a straightforward ploy to control through fear. What often goes unnoticed is the way the same strategy is used between adults. Most commentators now acknowledge, for example, that the Tories won the 1992 British General Election by successfully invoking the Labour Party bogey-men of higher taxes, economic mismanagement and prolonged union disputes. In a similar way some evangelicals try to frighten people into conformity by raising the spectre of liberalism.

'If you carry on talking like that', one well-known speaker was chided by a leading evangelical, 'people are going to think you've gone liberal, and before long, you'll find that you won't be seen as fully evangelical, and then doors are going to close and then . . .' 'I don't really give a monkey's!', the other man replied boldly, as he waved goodbye to a repeat invitation to that particular event. I applaud him. It really is time we stopped using meaningless labels, and boxing each other in with childish threats of bogey-men. It really is ridiculous that certain pulpits and platforms are only open to kosher evangelicals; so much needed input is lost this way. I am not saying that theology and doctrine are unimportant, far from it; but there is no evidence from the Bible that it is of ultimate importance. Doctrinal correctness matters little to God and labels matter less; honesty, openness and a sincere searching for truth, on the other hand, matter a great deal. Let me tell you a story about 'The Spring Harvest Speaker and the Liberal Bishop.'

Jesus told a parable to a gathering of evangelical leaders. 'A Spring Harvest speaker and a liberal bishop each sat down to read the Bible. The Spring Harvest speaker thanked God for the precious gift of the Holy Scriptures and pledged himself once again to proclaim them faithfully. "Thank you God", he prayed, "that I am not like this poor bishop who doesn't believe your word, and seems unable to make his mind up whether or not Christ rose from the dead." The bishop looked puzzled as he flicked through the pages of the Bible and said, "Virgin birth, water into wine, physical resurrection. I honestly don't know if I can believe these things Lord. In fact, I'm not even sure that I believe you exist as a personal Being, but I am going to keep on searching." I tell you that this liberal bishop rather than the other man went home justified before God. For everyone who thinks he has arrived at his destination has actually hardly begun, and he who continues searching is closer to his destination than he realizes.'

This version of the parable of the Pharisee and the tax collector is not a cheap jibe against Spring Harvest but an attempt to bring out the original point Jesus was making. It is a point which we so easily miss, since we stand at the end of a long Christian tradition in which pharisaism is seen as synonymous with self-righteousness and hypocrisy. The initial audience did not see it this way; they thought of a Pharisee as a man of great religious dedication and sincerity. By automatically seeing the Pharisee as the bad guy the true impact of the story is lost on us, and the parable serves only to reinforce our existing values and prejudices, whereas its original intention was to overturn them.[1] (It obviously follows that in a different setting – a gathering of liberal churchgoers, for example – the story might be told the other way round.)

God is ultimately unimpressed with our church pedigrees or our spiritual experiences or our credal affirmations. St Peter will not be asking us at the pearly gates which church we belonged to, or whether we believed in the virgin birth; the word 'evangelical' will not even enter the conversation. 'Liberal' no more determines that a person is not really Christian than 'evangelical' guarantees that somebody is a genuine Christian.

My contention is that neither standard-pack evangelicalism nor liberalism offers a very satisfying way forward, but before we look at my reasons for saying this, it may help to give a brief overview of how the present situation has come about.

The Parting of the Ways

It is widely acknowledged that somewhere around the late 1700s a major shift took place in Western culture, which is known as the Enlightenment. It basically came about as a reaction to feudalism, which had trapped people in ignorance and superstition. Feudal religion was straightforward: God was the big boss in the sky, and we humans were his subjects, who did his bidding without asking any questions. The church, which was his earthly seat of authority, determined the meaning of truth, not only in the realm of religion but in every other field as well: politics, science, history, art and so on. To dissent was to be branded a heretic and undergo persecution, excommunication or worse. Understandably, this period is generally thought of as 'pre-critical', in that there was no process of independent reasoning or questioning.

Then things began to change. René Descartes, one of the fathers of modern thought, sat down one chilly night and huddling up to the fire decided to question everything in his world, including his own existence. His momentous conclusion was that the act of doubting his own existence was the only demonstration that he did in fact exist, hence his famous dictum: *cogito ergo sum* ('I think therefore I am').[2] Modest though this declaration sounds, it actually shifted the whole basis of epistemology, or the way we know things, from the old certainties dictated by the church to a process of independent reason and doubt. The fact that Descartes had, so to speak, stepped out of himself and looked upon himself as an object, opened up the possibility of a completely different way of looking at the world. Rather than viewing it in a subjective way, as something to which one was inextricably connected, he had made it possible for the world to be looked at objectively, or in a detached way. The consequence was the beginning of objectivism, the modern scientific method by which things are examined dispassionately. The benefits which have flowed from this are fairly obvious, but as we shall see, there have been grave consequences too.

It might help those less familiar with the terms I am using to describe the development of Western culture, if I give a brief explanation of some of them.

- The eighteenth-century *Enlightenment* gave birth to what is known as *modernity*, or the modern outlook and the culture of the modern. *Modern* in this context means looking at the world in a *critical* way, or in a manner which takes nothing for granted. This approach is synonymous with the scientific method which seeks to research matters with objectivity, free from preconditions or dogma.
- The term *pre-modern* refers to the outlook which prevailed before the Enlightenment, and it is sometimes also called *pre-critical*, since the prevailing mythological and superstitious attitudes went virtually unchallenged.

- *Postmodernity* is the movement which has developed over the past couple of decades (although its roots go back much further), and which is in reaction to the exalted position modernity has given to reason and objectivism.

We could alternatively express this as:

Pre-modern	Modern	Post-modern
Pre-critical	Critical	Post-critical

Superstition	Reason	Intuition
Mythology	Demythologizing	Remythologizing

Obviously, religion was seriously affected by the Enlightenment and there was no way things could carry on as before. The toothpaste was out of the tube, so to speak, and no-one would be able to get it back in. During the nineteenth century, religious liberalism emerged as a bold attempt to synthesize the new way of thinking and what was deemed the essence of Christianity. The new approaches to history and the natural sciences seemed to make a naive belief in the Bible impossible, and liberalism rose to the challenge of modernizing the Christian religion. Biblical criticism flourished, drawing on all the latest methods of research. The Genesis account of creation naturally came under fire from Darwinism, and historical findings demonstrated the unlikelihood that many books of the Bible were written by their stated authors; even Jesus was subjected to investigation, as scholars searched for the 'historical Jesus' or the man behind the theological gloss of the New Testament.

Needless to say, conservative believers in all denominations reacted violently to what was perceived as the liberal sell-out to modernism, and a powerful back-lash ensued. Liberals saw no reason to treat the Bible any differently from any other ancient text, whereas the conservatives were scandalized at the thought of subjecting the word of God to human investigation. Fundamental doctrines such as the inerrancy of the Bible, the deity of Christ, the virgin birth, substitutionary atonement, the physical resurrection of Christ and his bodily return to earth, were staunchly defended as irreducible basics. The evangelical movement, especially in the United States, was at the heart of the debate, and it was from this camp that a coalition was formed in the early 1920s under the banner of 'fundamentalism'. In the following decades a bitter battle ensued between the fundamentalists and the liberals over who would gain the upper hand in the theological institutions and the denominational bureaucracies.[3]

Although fundamentalists have always been indisputably evangelicals, it became increasingly clear that not all evangelicals wanted to be seen as fundamentalists. By the early 1950s a group of respected scholars and a young evangelist called Billy Graham decided to distance themselves from fundamentalism, which was recognized as being anti-intellectual and overly defensive towards modern scholarship. Their stated intention was to create a 'new evangelical theology',[4] which could on the one hand stand apart from fundamentalism, while at the same time continue to maintain the same basic form of doctrine. Many contemporary evangelicals stand by a similar position. Indeed, thanks to the media image of fundamentalists and the increasing use of the term with respect to extremist elements in other faiths, hardly anyone now wants to be called 'fundamentalist'.

In the light of this brief overview of the historical conflict between evangelicalism and liberalism, we should now return to my earlier point, that neither of them offers a fully satisfactory way forward for many post-evangelicals. Why is this so?

The Evangelical Option

Evangelicalism has brought and continues to bring to the Christian church many good things, which no doubt will continue to be valued by post-evangelical people as well. There are many examples I could give of this, and I would like to pinpoint two of them. The first is a deep love of and respect for the Scriptures. In my own case, I was faithfully taught them from when I was a young boy, and there has never been a time in my life when I have felt that they did not matter, or when I have not been anxious to learn from them. Like so many others, I gained this love of Scripture from an evangelical heritage. But this is more than a knowledge of, or even a respect for, the Scriptures; evangelicalism brings an acute expectation that God will speak through them – they are the word of God. They do not exist primarily to be dissected and analysed; they exist as a sacrament, or a means of God communicating himself to us. I hope that post-evangelicals will never cease to approach the Bible both with diligence and with a listening ear.

The other thing I would like to mention that evangelicals have bequeathed to the wider church is a robust emphasis on the gospel as something that can be expressed in a simple form, and which challenges each and every one of us on a personal level. This is, of course, the legacy of the Reformation, but it is something which evangelicals have been particularly diligent in maintaining and preserving. There can be no doubt that the vast majority of people who convert to Christianity do so through the medium of the evangelical section of the church and this is clearly thanks to the faithfulness and simplicity with which evangelicals present the gospel. Post-evangelicals may well react to the over-simplification and, quite frankly, the crassness of much evangelism, but they must never lose sight of the centrality of the gospel and the importance of holding it out to a world which still needs it.

But of course there are also the downsides to evangelicalism, some of which, ironically, are linked to the strengths just mentioned. There is a tendency to make an idol out of the Bible. I believe it was the Argentinian preacher Juan Carlos Ortis, who spoke of St Evangelical worshipping a trinity of Father, Son and Holy Scripture. This is a quite valid comment, even though painful to bear. To some considerable degree this over-exalting of the Bible stems from evangelicalism's conflict with modernism in the late nineteenth century. It is true that the Reformation affirmed the uniqueness of Scripture – *sola Scriptura* – but that arose out of a quite different battle with catholicism's emphasis on papal authority and the authority of church tradition. While this is still relevant, the main battleground for evangelicals, with regard to the Bible, remains in the area of biblical criticism.

The simple fact is that there is a huge gulf between, on the one hand, evangelical scholarship, which largely accepts the necessity of biblical criticism, and seeks to utilize its insights and methods, and on the other hand evangelical churches where it is not uncommon to find an anti-critical attitude towards the Bible. Indeed, at a popular level this takes the form of burying one's head in the sand and declaring something like, 'Well I think we should just believe the Bible, don't you?' Granted, there may be a little bit more sophistication than this but, sadly, not much. Try talking in an average evangelical church about something like the 'synoptic problem' (the discrepancies between the accounts given in the first three Gospels), or suggesting that we do not really know who wrote the Fourth Gospel, or that the story of Jonah being swallowed by a whale might well be mythical in nature, and you will quickly see what I mean.

Closely tied in with this anti-criticism is a prevailing sense of certainty and absoluteness with regard to Christian things. A dominant theme I encountered when talking to people of a post-evangelical persuasion, in researching for this book, was their dismay at the lack of grey areas in evangelical churches: virtually everything comes across in black or white terms. And the places where people felt this was most obvious and blatant were the pulpits and the large platforms, where it was felt that preachers (especially charismatics) frequently denounced critical thinking as unbelief or as a tool of the devil. Although much of this anti-criticism surrounds the question of the Bible, it also shows up in the area of prayer. People sometimes thank God when prayers are 'answered', and either forget them or blame the devil when they are not answered. I find it particularly irritating when someone says, 'The Lord was really good to me on Monday . . .' because I always want to say, 'Oh and I suppose he was really awful to you on Tuesday and Wednesday.' Then there are the people who say, 'So the Lord said to me . . .' Even with my best efforts to suspend my critical faculties, I cannot believe that God speaks to people in such a clearcut, matter of fact way – especially when it apparently happens before and after every cup of tea!

The Liberal Option

The irritation lots of people feel with the anti-critical tendencies within evangelicalism certainly provides some incentive to look down the liberal road. Many people pick up books by liberal authors or look at materials produced by the Student Christian Movement, for example, and find them quite stimulating. The SCM's recent publication _No More Mr Nice Guy_,[5] which explores different perspectives on the person of Jesus, has been used to very great effect at Holy Joe's, as I know it has elsewhere. Another recent publication which some of us have found very helpful is the book _Liberal Evangelism_ by John Saxbee, the Bishop of Ludlow.[6] This is an honest and stimulating attempt to show the need for a liberal contribution to the Decade of Evangelism. Probably the most appealing aspect of liberalism for post-evangelicals is its spirit of openness. Given that they have found evangelicalism very prepacked and conservative, the air of liberalism feels fresh and bracing.

I think it is fair to say, however, that liberalism has had its fundamentalist element as well. John Saxbee illustrates this by contrasting two distinct approaches to liberalism. The first one by S.W. Sykes is what I would call a liberal-fundamentalist approach:

Liberalism in theology is that mood or cast of mind which is prepared to accept that some discovery of reason may count *against* the authority of a traditional affirmation in the body of Christian theology. One is a theological liberal if one allows autonomously functioning reason to supply arguments against traditional beliefs and if one's reformulation of Christian belief provides evidence that one has ceased to believe what has been traditionally believed by Christians.

Sykes has chosen to define his brand of liberalism in a very negative and doctrinaire fashion. He in fact demonstrates that some aspects of liberalism have been as much influenced and shaped by their conflict with conservative Christianity, as the conservatives have by their conflict with liberalism. He actually states that one is a liberal *if* one allows reason to supply arguments *against* traditional beliefs.

John Habgood, who has described himself as a conservative liberal, comes across in a quite different way:

> . . . for me [liberalism] represents an openness in the search for truth which I believe is profoundly necessary for the health of religion. We grow in knowledge, only insofar as we are prepared to criticise what we think and know already. True knowledge is tested knowledge, just as true faith has to be sifted with doubt . . . . Openness in the search for truth also entails a positive, but again critical, approach to secular knowledge. . . . It is essentially about honesty, but an honesty rooted in what God has given us, both in revelation and in the created world.

I am sure that post-evangelicals, and many thoroughgoing evangelicals, will respond to the positiveness of Habgood's approach. He uses altogether different language: words like 'honesty', 'openness' and 'search for truth'. It is also heartening that he takes a positive *yet critical* approach to secular knowledge. One need not agree with Habgood on many other issues in order to appreciate his method and attitude, expressed in this extract.

There are two reasons, however, why post-evangelicals are unlikely to slither down the slippery slopes of liberalism. The first and most pressing is simply that they are post-evangelicals. That is, their evangelical background still counts for quite a lot. Evangelicalism may prove frustrating in lots of ways, but it did help bring them to faith in the first place, and the importance of personal salvation remains crucial. They also accept (perhaps critically) that the Christ-event is based on historical realities, and they have no real difficulty with the supernatural nature of the gospel and the possibility of miracles. The Bible plays a normative part in their understanding of doctrine and practical Christian living, and they readily affirm the Apostles' Creed.

Two Sides of the Same Coin

There is arguably a better reason, however, why neither evangelicalism as it is commonly experienced nor liberalism offers an ideal way forward, and this is that they actually have something in common: they both find their natural cultural roots in modernity. This may appear more obvious with respect to liberals than it does to evangelicals, yet it is equally true for them too, if even in the negative sense, that their faith has been influenced by its conflict with liberalism.

An obvious way in which this could be seen is in the way that evangelicals join liberals in accepting the same basic reference point of modern scientific knowledge. To a large degree liberalism exists because of its acceptance of modern scientific knowledge as the final arbiter for determining truth. So I need say no more about that. But evangelicalism effectively does just the same in that it chooses to fight the modernist challenge by using the framework and criteria provided by modernism. Evangelicals are often accused of taking the Bible literally; this is not really the case. Increasingly they oscillate between literal and non-literal interpretations. Far from being arbitrary, this oscillation is controlled by the need to defend an ideological stance that the Bible contains no real errors. With the increase of scientific knowledge, the Bible has to be continually reinterpreted in order to maintain its credibility. The most obvious example concerns the Genesis account of creation. As many leading evangelicals accept that it is now impossible, from a scientific point of view, to insist that the world was created in six twenty-four-hour days, they choose to reinterpret the meaning of 'days' as geological ages, rather than literal days, and in this way the Bible's credibility is protected. Many other such examples could be given to demonstrate the same point.[7]

As we shall see in a moment, the objectivism of the scientific outlook is now undergoing serious assault; indeed, the whole notion of objectivism is under attack. Objectivity is still something to be sought, but the idea of objectivism – the belief that there is such a thing as entirely objective knowledge *which is accessible to us* – seems to be disappearing. As you might expect, this point is hotly disputed, but if we pretend that there is a ready future for objectivism, we are deceiving ourselves. One of the fiercest attacks on objectivism in respect to theology has been mounted by the American theologian Walter Wink.[8] After immersing himself for many years in the liberal academy he took on the pastorate of a church, where he discovered the enormous gulf between the sophistication of his learning and the actual needs of ordinary people. After a long search Wink became convinced of the need for a theology and a spiritual life which, whilst incorporating the fruits of the critical age, press on to a more holistic consciousness than objective knowledge alone can achieve.[9] What he describes is actually post-critical, or postmodern (some would say postliberal, but at this point, I am in serious danger of contracting post-itus!) – and I am convinced that this is where the future lies for post-evangelicals.

6 'Let Me Tell You a Story'

We have already touched on the subject of postmodernism and we now need to look at this a little more closely. I have referred several times to the fact that the Western world is in a state of flux and that the modern world, stretching back to the Enlightenment, is now crumbling. It has far from disappeared and is unlikely to do so for a very long time, but serious cracks are growing in all directions, and out of the cracks of this crumbling culture a new postmodern world is emerging. It is a world which understands itself through biological rather than mechanistic models; a world where people see themselves as belonging to the environment, rather than over it or apart from it; a world distrustful of institutions, hierarchies, centralized bureaucracies and male dominated organizations. It is a world in which networks and local grass-roots activities take precedence over large-scale structures and grand designs; a world in which the book age is giving way to the screen age; a world hungry for spirituality, yet dismissive of systematized religion.[1] It is a world in which image and reality are so deeply intertwined that it is difficult to draw the line between the two.[2]

Those who think that postmodernism is a figment of the academic imagination, a passing intellectual fad, could not be more wrong. Postmodernism has flowed right out of the musty corridors of academia into the world of popular culture; it is on the pages of youth magazines, on CD boxes and the fashion pages of *Vogue*.[3] It has abolished the old distinction between 'high' and 'low' art, and created new art forms out of things like music videos, urban graffiti and computer graphics. Few things could, in fact, sum up the postmodern situation better than the term 'virtual reality', for it is a world in which the old certainties are dissolving.

My thesis is simple: that post-evangelicals tend to be people who identify culturally more with postmodernity (the culture of the postmodern) than with modernity, and that this has a significant bearing on the way that they approach and understand the Christian faith. I am not suggesting that they accept blindly whatever the new culture throws at them; indeed, one of the greatest challenges facing post-evangelicals is the task of undertaking a critique of the world they inhabit, and deciding what is and what is not amenable to the Christian faith.

A World of Different Stories

One of the most helpful ways of thinking about the distinction between the worlds of the modern and the postmodern is to think of them as stories or narratives – versions of reality. The modern or Enlightenment version of reality, which for a long time has been the 'authorised' version, can be thought of as a 'big' story or epic, which tries to tell us everything. It not only tells us how things are but how they were and how they should be; it explains the whole thing – from a particular angle. Such stories abounded in the nineteenth century as the modernist worldview flourished. Darwin gave us the story of the evolution of species, Marx the story of social conflict, Freud the story of the inner world of the human psyche. Big stories, or meta-narratives as they are sometimes called, are very appealing; they offer security with their 'once upon a time' and their 'happily ever after'. But what happens when the endings no longer seem plausible? Or when the storyteller loses his thread? What happens when the writer's hidden agenda begins to show? Or when we realize that they are *just* stories, or convincing versions of reality, rather than reality itself? For this is what is happening in our world: the big stories and the storytellers are losing credibility and fewer people want to gather around to listen.[4]

There is a consensus that this disillusionment with the great 'epics' of modernity can be traced back as far as World War I, which, with its unspeakable horrors, shattered the dream that scientific man could grasp his own destiny and create a utopia. Add to this the Holocaust and the bombings of Hiroshima and Nagasaki and all the terrors which have followed, and it is quite clear that the big epics have run out of credible storylines.[5] And it is not just the scientific and technological stories which have lost credibility; the political and religious tales are proving even less believable. What happens when the modern world loses its romance? When dreams of 'progress for the common good of humankind' turn into nightmares like Bosnia and Rwanda? We find the following taking place:

- People turn away from big stories to more modest 'episodes'. In other words, they are suspicious of large-scale explanations and universal moralities.

Truth is what you find out for yourself, not what someone else imposes on you.

- People are suspicious of certainty and distrust claims of objectivity; the world is a much more blatantly subjective place.
- We enter an age of pluralism and relativism. It is perfectly valid for you to have your story, your version of truth, just so long as you do not try to force it on anyone else. The unforgivable sin is to behave as though you have cornered the market on truth.
- The tendency is to 'mix and match' from all sorts of different sources – you patch together your own stories or your own versions of truth, drawing on things new and old.
- There is a search for spirituality, though seldom through the channels of conventional religion. Religious big stories are no more appealing than any others.

This is the postmodernist version of reality. Zygmunt Bauman, a leading sociologist, describes it as 'modernity without illusions'.[6] In other words, its claims are much more modest; it no longer says 'Here is the truth – believe it!' It says, 'Try this for size.'

As I have said, this is no academic gobbledygook: it is the real world. People may not label it as academics do; they may not even be aware of what is happening, but happening it surely is. The important question is: what do we make of it? Is it good, bad or indifferent from a Christian perspective? One thing is certain: it poses an entirely new interpretative situation for Christianity; and as the American theologian Walter Brueggemann points out, the evangelical church in the West is decidedly unprepared for the task of reinterpreting its faith.[7] Why? Because it is lodged in a cultural time-warp, still interpreting its faith in the language and ideas of the 'big story'. This is understandable: evangelicalism has had over a hundred years of dealings with the world of the big story. But it is time to move on. The old certainties are passing away, and we can no longer assume that there is some objective basis of truth that everyone accepts. As Brueggemann says, all claims to reality are under negotiation, and theology can no longer make absolute claims in a vacuum and expect a ready acceptance.[8]

For those whose roots are in the culture of the big story, all this probably sounds either outrageous, scary – or both. They may wonder whether there can possibly be any place for Christianity in postmodernism. Brueggemann is quite sure there is. Indeed, he believes that the Christian community has unique resources with which to fund this new cultural situation. Reality is no longer the fixed arrangement of the scientific era, he tells us; this is actually a considerably more hospitable situation to spiritual and theological possibilities. But such possibilities cannot be put forward in absolutist terms. We can take a full part in negotiating the future of our culture, provided we neither pretend to be 'privileged insiders' – people who know the truth with certainty – nor allow ourselves to be 'trivialized outsiders'.[9]

The Dawning of a New Age

The dark side of postmodernism is very dark. Zygmunt Bauman says it is marked by an 'all-deriding, all-eroding, all-dissolving destructiveness'.[10] Its ability to deconstruct all the old certainties plunges us into a sea of confusion in which nothing is quite clear anymore. But Bauman sees this as a site-clearing operation, and he speaks of its power to 're-enchant' all that modernity tried hard to 'dis-enchant'. What does he mean? Modernity, he says, was all about the declaration of reason's independence; rationalism and objectivism had to take precedence over all else. It was nothing short of a 'war against mystery and magic', he asserts, and in order for rationalism to win, 'the world had to be de-spiritualised, de-animated, denied the capacity of the subject.' In this scheme of things the earth became a repository of 'natural resources', and we ended up with timber instead of forests and waterways instead of lakes. 'It is against such a disenchanted world', Bauman says, 'that the postmodern re-enchantment is aimed';[11] dignity can once again be returned to emotions, there is respect for ambiguity, and 'mystery is no longer a barely tolerated alien, awaiting a deportation order.' It is no longer emotions and spiritual things which are mistrusted but cold and calculating reason.[12]

The New Age movement is obviously a classic way in which Bauman's descriptions are being fulfilled. Indeed, Graham Cray speaks of the New Age movement as a postmodern paradigm or model. It is said to be the fastest growing spiritual movement in the world today, and despite the near-hysterical reactions to it from so many evangelicals (and Catholics) John Drane has given his book the title, *What is the New Age Saying to the Church?* He gives a convincing picture of the way in which New Age attitudes, practices and styles are flooding the Western world (though seldom with a New Age label), and he is sure that if we fail to enter into constructive engagement with the questions being raised within the movement, we will reinforce the dominant, negative image that most Westerners already have of the church.[13] It offers an incredible opportunity,

> Simply because never before in modern times have so many people been aware of spiritual realities. Rapidly increasing numbers are finding it possible to believe in reincarnation, spirit guides, and extra-terrestrials, and all sorts of other esoteric ideas. To traditional Christians, this might be unfamiliar terri-tory. But it certainly means that these people are spiritually open as no other generation within living memory has been. All New Agers are winnable for Christ. In the case of every New Ager I have met, I have felt that God could give that person to the church as a gift, if only he or she could meet Chris-tians in whose lives the reality of Christ was an everyday experience.[14]

Without doubt, the scientific, materialist worldview which has dominated the Western world, is collapsing, and the atheistic materialism of the Eastern bloc coun-tries has already collapsed. This is an exciting new era which is dawning, an entirely new interpretative situa-tion, but its challenge is not simply on the level of mission; it reaches deep into our own self-consciousness as Christians and human beings; it delves deep into the foundations of our faith: the way we understand truth, the Bible, and even God. It is nothing less than 'the deep interrogation of every breathing aspect of lived experience'.[15]

'Is Yours a Flat-Pack?'

Walter Brueggemann tells us that in this new situation preachers must not yield to the temptation to offer a full alternative world; postmodernity is characterized by its imagination, and our task is to fund that imagination: to provide the pieces, materials and resources out of which a new world can be imagined. 'Our responsibility', he says, 'is not a grand scheme or a coherent system, but the voicing of a lot of little pieces out of which people can put life together in fresh configurations.' We must make available 'lots of disordered pieces that admit more than one large ordering'.[16]

Transformation is the goal of the gospel and this has been approached in the past by presenting a whole fixed doctrinal and moral scheme expressed within a definite cultural form. In other words, it has been offered in the form of one particular model. I can illustrate this by saying that it has come like a flat-pack piece of furniture. When you open the box, you find a collection of various components and an instruction sheet which lists the pieces and shows a finished item. Sadly the instructions generally leave you somewhat bewildered as to how to make it all fit together, but there is scope for a little variation, insofar as you can leave out or add in some of the peripheral bits. But there is only one thing you can make out of it.

From my observation, post-evangelicals are more at ease with a meccano set which still has a basic set of components but which offers you an instruction book full of different possible models which can be constructed – some more basic and others highly elaborate. You can even branch out and imagine some other models of your own. If that sounds too relativistic, or too much as if 'anything goes', it is worth pondering further. There are restrictions: you only have that set of pieces and they will only fit together in certain ways. You cannot mix meccano with lego, for example. Perhaps this illustration matches Paul's contention in Galatians. The believers at Galatia were being sold a 'flat-pack' in the form of rigid legalism; he exhorted them to stick with the meccano set of freedom in Christ. The essential 'pieces' to be constructed were the fruits of the Spirit (Galatians 5.22–3) and provided they were not mixed with the 'works of the flesh' (19–21) they could be formed in a million configurations of human potential and imagination. Rather than seeing the Bible as a big picture of a single fixed model, we should look on it as a resource book, which 'funds' our imaginative venture with basic pieces and offers us many different models. The result is plurality without a necessary collapse into pluralism and relativity, without sinking into the 'anything goes' of relativism.

If this sounds far too risky, Brueggeman assures us that the threat of remaining stuck in our rigid frameworks of certainty is far greater. I guess the problem is one of security. But the time has come for us to climb out of the little boat of our settled certainties and join Jesus in walking on the waters of uncertainty and vulnerability. As the German ecologist Rudolph Bahro says, 'When the forms of an old culture are dying, the new culture is created by a few people who are not afraid to be insecure.'[17]

7 The Truth, the Whole Truth, and Something Quite Like the Truth

You may have heard about 'paradigm shifts'. If not, let me tell you about a trick with a pack of cards. Thomas Kuhn, the man who came up with the idea of paradigm shifts, tells of an experiment involving a pack of cards with a difference: the pack contained some 'strange' cards, like a red six of spades and a black four of hearts. The subjects of the experiment were asked to identify cards from the pack (including the strange ones) as they were shown to them in rapid succession. All the subjects initially perceived the strange cards incorrectly, but as the exposure time lengthened they became confused because they knew the categories they were placing them in were wrong, yet they neither knew why nor what to do about it. With further lengthening of exposure time, most of the subjects realized that this or that card was the wrong colour, and after a few more goes they could accurately identify all the cards. A few of the subjects, however, just could not make the necessary adjustment; even when the exposure time was increased by forty times that normally needed to recognize a card, more than 10 per cent of the strange cards were not correctly identified. These subjects then became deeply distressed; one of them exclaimed, 'I can't make the suit out, whatever is it. It didn't even look like a card that time. I don't know what colour it is now or whether it's a spade or a heart. I'm not even sure now what a spade looks like. My God!'[1]

Kuhn, whose field of study was science, became convinced that research of any sort takes place within a paradigm, which we could describe as the whole cluster of beliefs and values which are taken for granted within a given community. It is probably simplest to think of it as a 'school of thought'. All progress made within that community is going to be linked to, indeed determined by, its controlling paradigm. The questions which are asked, or not asked, within that particular field of activity will obviously be dependent on what is taken for granted and consequently, some areas of research will just not be opened up. It is a bit like looking through a window and getting a 'frame' on the reality which lies beyond. You are unlikely to enquire about specific things which lie outside of the field of vision from the window, for the obvious reason that the question will not arise using that particular frame.

Because no paradigm is perfect or complete, problems inevitably arise: anomalies or inconsistencies which the paradigm cannot process. When too many anomalies arise, the paradigm goes into crisis, and there are three possible outcomes: first, the anomalies are tackled and resolved within the paradigm; second, they may not be solved but since no alternative paradigm emerges which can solve them, the problems are simply put on the back burner; or third, no solutions appear but there is a shift to a new paradigm, so that the anomalies become irrelevant and progress continues using the new paradigm. If too many problems are put on the back burner, the credibility of the paradigm sinks rapidly and an even bigger crisis occurs. One other point worth noting is that, according to Kuhn, the shift to a new paradigm does not take place through a straightforward logical development, but through an inspired and imaginative leap; in other words, the 'conversion' involves a substantial intuitive element.[2] You hardly need me to explain the whole host of possible parallels which this model yields in terms of tensions and developments which occur within the church.

The playing cards experiment, which illustrates the difficulty and confusion which arises when people become aware of anomalies, offers a good description of what many post-evangelicals experience. Initially, they just have vague feelings of discomfort about various things in their evangelical church: the constant chorus-singing bores them or the dogmatic tone of sermons irritates them. Soon the bigger issues underneath the surface irritations begin to crystallize and the credibility of the paradigm is in serious jeopardy. Before long they decide that the survival of their faith may depend on finding some new categories or perspectives with which they can make sense of it. Sadly, some react like the minority in the card experiment, and become increasingly confused and stressed by the lack of satisfactory resolution. Frequently they either fall by the wayside or become convinced that the problem is within themselves and go through long periods of sadness or depression.

Post-evangelicalism is what takes place when people find that they have shifted paradigms and they no longer relate to the old evangelical paradigm. Their reference points and the things they take for granted have changed; to use my earlier illustration, they have found a different and, for them, a better 'window' on reality. In my view the central issue in this paradigm shift has to do with the nature of truth; it is a move away from the sense of certainty which characterizes evangelicalism, to an understanding of truth as something more provisional and symbolic, and therefore less able to be put into hard and fast statements. The implications of such a change of consciousness are clearly immense.

'It's Not *what* You Know – It's the *Way* that You Know It'

Nothing is more fundamental to a paradigm than its epistemology or its theory of knowledge – how truth is established. For evangelicals, truth is a very clearcut issue: something is either true in a fairly literal or historical way or it is not true at all. Post-evangelicals, on the other hand, feel uneasy with such a cut and dried approach and find themselves instinctively drawn towards an understanding of truth which is more relative. This is naturally interpreted by fellow evangelicals as a sell-out to secular or liberal forces and they are soon saying things like 'But the Bible says . . .' or 'We mustn't compromise on God's standards' or 'The truth is the truth, and we mustn't try to change it' the assumption being that the person is deliberately playing fast and loose with what they know to be right. From an epistemological perspective this may be a long way from what is really happening. The issue is probably more to do with differences of comprehension or perception. Or to put it another way, it is not so much a matter of differences of opinion as differences in the way opinions are reached.

Another way of thinking about this, is to recognize two types of language: scientific language and poetic language.[3] Behind each of these two types of language lie quite distinct ways of comprehending reality. The distinction could be expressed as follows

Scientific Language	Poetic Language
Precise	Imprecise
Permanent	Provisional
Absolute	Ambiguous
Propositional	Approximate
Rational	Intuitive
Literal	Symbolic

(Naturally, in this context 'scientific' and 'poetic' are not necessarily referring to actual science or poetry, but to ways of looking at and understanding reality.)

It is well recognized that language is ambiguous: words and sentences have a multiplicity of possible meanings. Scientific language always aims to eliminate these ambiguities and leave us with precise and absolute statements, while poetic language delights in ambiguity and even plays with it quite deliberately. From the point of view of the modern world, scientific language is considered greatly superior when it comes to discussing 'real' things; poetic language has its place and is fine for poets, but it lacks the stability for dealing with objective truths.

Postmodernity, however, is bringing about an entirely new interpretative situation in which, as I have already stressed, the very notion of objectivism is under serious threat. As Richard Rorty, a postmodern thinker, puts it: objectivity is just a matter of agreement of everyone in the room,[4] the problem being that only certain types of people have been allowed in the room who are, for the most part, white middle-class males. We might say that postmodernity is what happens when marginalized peoples refuse to keep quiet anymore, and the result is the emergence of a whole new consciousness, which, while embracing the need for objectivity, insists that non-rational perception is of equal importance; that ambiguity, feelings and intuition provide real information too.

Looking at these two types of language and their underlying forms of perception, it is clear that evangelicalism frames its concept of truth in the form of scientific language, and that this has a significant effect on the way the Bible is treated. It might be argued that evangelicalism also accommodates plenty of feelings, emotions and intuitive insights. The whole nineteenth-century style of preaching the gospel, for example, which still strongly influences evangelistic presentations, leans heavily on emotive techniques of appeal. Then there is the charismatic dimension which has standardized contributions of the 'I just feel the Lord is saying . . .' variety; there are prophecies and pictures and 'laughing in the Spirit', yet none of this fundamentally affects the very absolutist fashion in which truth is conceived. Even what might be called the pre-modern elements of evangelicalism are understood and expressed in an absolutist, 'scientific' manner. Take the emphasis on spiritual warfare, for instance. Descriptions of territorial spirits controlling towns and cities, and accounts of 'clearing the atmosphere' through prayer and praise marches, all have a distinctly medieval ring about them, and yet they are spoken of in a rational, matter-of-fact way by distinctly modern people, as though they were talking about dusting away cobwebs from the lounge window or vacuum-cleaning the bedroom.

My contention is that the shift from evangelical to post-evangelical is not primarily about surface culture, about moral standards or styles of worship; it is first and foremost about a difference in perception of truth. Influenced to some degree by the cultural development from modern to postmodern, a post-evangelical consciousness of truth is to be found less in propositional statements and moral certitudes and more in symbols, ambiguities and situational judgments. Not that this necessarily makes it less true, or its followers less passionate to know what is true. Indeed the opposite might be argued to be the case: that when truth remains a fixed certitude, people tend to take it for granted and fail to think it through for themselves, whereas if absolute truth is seen to be always a step beyond human grasp, the need for people to think for themselves and engage in a persistent search becomes much stronger. This is certainly borne out by my own observations. When visitors to Holy Joe's have complained about the level of open-ended questioning they see taking place, I usually suggest that at least these people are searching for truth and struggling with some degree of honesty to find a faith they can believe in, rather than just taking it for granted.

'Is There Anybody There?'

One of the most significant factors underlying the debate about truth, is the role of language. Deconstructionism, a method of linguistic criticism developed by people like the French philosopher Jacques Derrida, questions the premise that there are real entities outside language to which language refers. We are all aware of the difficulties involved in communicating religious ideas and concepts to people outside our particular faith community; what deconstructionists ask is whether there is anything out there in the first place.

It must surely be conceded that a great deal of religious language is vacuous. Phrases like 'the Lord told me . . .', 'God is at work in the situation' and 'the devil's really been having a go at me' are all a standard part of many people's day-to-day vocabulary, yet they often need decoding as ways of saying something else like 'I want you to listen to what I'm saying', or 'Things are going well', or 'Things are going badly'. Of course, we are all guilty of meaningless religious talk from time to time, but the question posed by deconstructionism is much more disturbing than this. It asks whether *any* of our talk about God (even the sensible stuff) actually makes sense.

Don Cupitt, the radical theologian, responds with a firm 'No'. As he sees it, all talk of God is little more than a sophisticated fairy tale. In a reversal of one of Plato's stories, Cupitt asks us to imagine ourselves living in a cave from which there is no escape. All we can do is enlarge the cave, which is surrounded by impenetrable rock, as dark as night. We never go outside the cave and nothing ever enters. We never see a dawn or feel a breeze. Within the cave we tell each other stories about the life beyond in order to stave off the inevitable truth – that there is nothing outside. All the old religious certainties are being dispersed across the sea of language, Cupitt tells us, and language is all self-referential: it does not refer to anything outside itself. If you look up a word in the dictionary, you will simply be referred to other words; and when you look up those words you are referred to still other words, and so on. Finally, there are only words, he tells us, vast proliferating systems of signs. It is useless to look for meaning outside language, it does not exist. When we speak of God we are just attempting to bring meaning into a situation which is ultimately meaningless.[5]

Of course it can then be argued that Cupitt's chilling tale of nihilistic emptiness is itself just a story; and it certainly is not the only outcome of deconstructionist theory. Derrida, whose thought has considerably influenced Cupitt, denies that the non-realist route is inevitable. 'I never cease to be surprised', he says, 'by critics who see my work as a declaration that there is nothing beyond language, that we are imprisoned in language; it is in fact saying the exact opposite.'[6] What it is doing, however, is challenging the traditional assumptions about the referential nature of language, that is to say, the notion that we can easily and accurately use language to refer to entities outside language. From the point of view of our discussion it does this in two ways: first, it shows us the all-pervasiveness of language – that we have no way of stepping outside language and proving that something is objectively true; and second, it shows us the immense difficulty of defining meaning in an unambiguous way. The reason for this is that the only way we can talk about something outside language is by using metaphors and models or the like. The problem that deconstructionism has highlighted is that as soon as we analyse or deconstruct metaphorical language it inevitably reveals inherent contradictions. We will think about this point in a little more detail.

The God who is There

We should emphasize that what deconstructionism cannot do is to prove that there is no God; what it can and does do is to reveal the difficulties of affirming that there is. In other words, we have to begin with a presupposition, based either on a given faith commitment or deliberate unbelief. Cupitt has opted for a particular version of radical unbelief, but it is equally acceptable to choose to believe. Initially, that decision to believe will probably be based on a gut reaction, which is fine provided we are then prepared to test it out and arrive at a place whereby we have satisfied ourselves that faith is a reasonable position to take. Since that probably takes us on to the subject of a different book, we shall settle for commenting on the difficulties that arise once we have settled for the fact that there is an external reality called God.

A great deal hinges here on the sort of understanding we have of metaphor. Historically metaphors have been understood as figures of speech, or colourful ways of saying something which could easily be put more plainly. Nowadays we recognize the situation to be rather more complicated than this; we now know that metaphors are an essential part of the way we grasp reality; in other words, they yield real information, which cannot necessarily be gained or understood in any other way. At one level a metaphor is nonsense. To say, for example, that 'time flies' is silly: time does not have wings; we cannot even say that time passes at different speeds on different occasions, and yet the idea of time flying is both emotive and very revealing. It makes one think of having fun, and then suddenly realizing what the time is; or being in a panic to get something done and realizing that time is 'running out'. For a metaphor to work, or yield some information, it has to have a tension at its very heart; it walks a narrow pathway between sense and nonsense. This tension can actually be located in the verb 'to be', which properly contains an 'is/is not'.[7] So we would need to say, 'time does/does not fly'. Or more to the point for our purposes, 'God is/is not a heavenly father'.

A serious problem, certainly, at the popular level of evangelicalism is that metaphors to describe God or the unseen spiritual realm are treated in much too literal a manner; it is assumed that 'father' really is a description of God rather than a metaphor, that when the Bible talks of God getting angry, or rejoicing, it actually means it in a human or near-human way. Linguistically we could say that this amounts to abandoning the tension in the metaphor, which consequently ceases to be a depiction of truth and sinks into a crude description of truth.

Although some of the questions that theology now faces are new, the issues go way back, and the problems associated with attempts to describe God have long been understood by theologians. As far back as the fifth century, a tension was recognized between two types of theology: the *via negativa* and the *via positiva*. *Via negativa* is a way of talking about God which recognizes straightaway the impossibility of properly describing or conceptualizing God in human terms. From this perspective, anthropomorphisms (which describe God in terms usually applied to human beings) are seen to be deceptions, which can easily lead to forms of idolatry. *Via negativa*, then, is always to be seen as primary, since it emphasizes the entire 'otherness' of a transcendent God. Having established this, we can then move towards *via positiva*, the form of theology which affirms features of God's person. The basis of this lies in the idea that the Creator has revealed something of himself in creation and in humanity in particular. The highest human qualities are therefore seen to be pointers to God, even though they are not descriptions.[8] Karl Barth actually insisted that the only way we can speak of God is in a *via dialectica*, or through an opposition of statement and counterstatement, of 'yes' and 'no', of paradox, in which the extremes of negative and positive are held together in the response of faith. This way of looking at God is emphasizing that he transcends any rational comprehension and, ultimately, any dogmatic formulation.[9] As you will appreciate, this negative/positive tension runs closely parallel to the metaphoric tension we have just spoken about. None of this suggests that our language to describe God is untrue or meaningless; indeed, we might argue that poetic language is more true and more meaningful than 'precise' or unambiguous scientific language.

One other perspective might prove useful. Assuming we opt for theological realism, that is, the belief that there is a real external entity called God, there are two roads we can travel down: that of naive realism or that of critical realism. *Naive realism* builds on the assumption that there is little or no difficulty in describing God or the spiritual dimension in a literal or near-literal way, pretty much as we speak of everyday objects and experiences. This is the overwhelmingly dominant understanding to be found at a popular level in evangelical churches. As we have been saying, if the Bible says that God gets angry or rejoices, or if it tells us that he is a father or a king, then that is fairly much the way it is. In other words, naive realism corresponds directly to what we earlier called 'scientific language'; hence truth is quite capable of being precise, absolute, literal and propositional, and of course the Bible is the repository of such truth. From this standpoint the Bible is expected to be entirely accurate historically: 'If we can't believe that Jonah was swallowed by a whale, then how can we believe that Jesus rose from the dead!'

In her excellent book *Metaphor and Religious Language* Janet Martin Soskice dismisses naive realism, saying that it is the legacy of literalism which equates religious truth with historical facts:

> Christianity is indeed a religion of the book, but not a book of this sort of fact. Its sacred texts are chronicles of experience, armouries of metaphor, and purveyors of an interpretative tradition. The sacred literature thus both records experiences of the past and provides the descriptive language by which any new experience may be interpreted. . . . All the metaphors which we use to speak to God arise from experiences of that which cannot be described, of that which Jews and Christians believe to be 'He who is'.[10]

I should stress that this does not mean that the Bible is devoid of historical content, but it does mean that our faith need not hinge on everything in the Bible being historically factual.

Critical realism is a concept used widely in the context of scientific theory, and it simply affirms the fact that there are many entities which, while they are non-observable, are nevertheless real – electric, magnetic and gravitational fields, for example. In a way they are transcendent, they are beyond our direct observation, hence the only access we have to them is through the use of models or metaphors. When we speak of a gravitational field, we know that there is no actual field; and yet the metaphor does refer to an actual reality, and what is more it informs us as to the nature of that reality. We could say that while models are not literally true, they are truth-depicting and truth-conveying.

From this perspective we can look at a metaphor such as the fatherliness of God and say that it has absolutely nothing to do with gender or biology; that what it discloses of God is his personhood and his nurture, love and care for creation. This argument has, of course, been at the heart of the debate over women's ordination. Opponents claim that if God is revealed in masculine form and has chosen male priests in the Old Testament to represent him, he clearly cannot be properly represented by a woman. But this argument is surely leaning too heavily on the 'is' side of the metaphor and losing sight of the 'is not' or the 'otherness' of God which cannot be contained in either masculine or feminine images. In itself this does not prove the case for either women's ordination or addressing God as mother, but it certainly demonstrates the different way in which some people approach the subject.

In summary, then, we can say that while a theory such as deconstructionism cannot tell us that God does not exist, it does enable us to recognize three things about our God-talk:

– It is impossible to escape from language and objectively say whether what we believe is true or not. Faith cannot be bypassed.

– Human language is unable to describe the external realities of God with any precision. As we have seen, this does not make language useless; it simply means that we have to accept its limitations.

– Religious language or talk about God and the spiritual realm is therefore inherently provisional and approximate in nature.

Where does this leave us with the concept of absolute truth? Most evangelicals use the term 'absolute truth' without ever considering its viability. I recently led a discussion in which a student bemoaned the difficulty of convincing people about the 'absolute truth of Christianity'. When I asked why he thought he needed to defend such a concept, he shrugged his shoulders and said, 'Well that's what Christianity is about isn't it? Absolute truth.' Let us ponder that point in the light of our discussion so far. If absolute truth is synonymous with the being of God, and he is entirely 'other' than ourselves, how are we going to gain access to such truth? If we thought that we did have such access, how could we know that we had, when we cannot escape language to test it out in an objective way? If our language is inherently ambiguous in its attempts to describe external realities and therefore unable to contain unequivocal truth, how can we refer to any truth as absolute? The concept is just not useful to us.

The Symbolism of the Cross

As an example of critical realism in practice, we can look at the subject of the atonement. Absolutely central to Christianity, the death of Christ is drenched in symbolism which draws on various Old Testament themes. Theologically, the atonement has always been understood with the help of models, and many such models have been put forward. The vast majority of evangelicals understand it through some kind of legal model, which says something like this: humankind is separated from God by sin, the only way that his righteousness could be satisfied and our sins forgiven was through a legal sacrifice which was without blemish, offered on our behalf. Jesus was that sacrifice, and through the shedding of his blood we can now be cleansed and brought back to God. There are many variations on this theme but these are the essential elements.

Many people have questioned this interpretation of Christ's death, on all kinds of different levels, and Don Cupitt, as might be expected, attacks it with vehemence. Along with various other doctrines, such as eternal torment and arbitrary election, Cupitt insists that the doctrine of atonement places God in a dubious light and makes him appear morally inferior to the creatures he made. God appears fickle, vengeful and morally underhanded according to Cupitt, who boldly announced that he was 'taking leave' of this sort of God notion.[11] I cannot imagine that there is a single Christian who has attempted to share his faith with others and who has not faced similar accusations against God from those he or she has tried to convert.

From a critical realist point of view, much of the problem comes from taking metaphoric language to be real and actual. But there are alternative interpretations. Let us consider one which is put forward by Stephen Ross White.[12] The first question to ask is what exactly was to be achieved through Christ's death and what is supposed to have changed through it. The traditional reply is that sins were cancelled out, forgiveness was granted, and therefore God's attitude towards us changed from wrath to mercy. The problems here are various and Cupitt is right to expose the poor light in which they place God. White's version agrees that reconciliation was the goal, but states that it was achieved through the demonstration of God's love, which *always* forgives, rather than through a once-for-all event of forgiveness. What is changed, then, is not God's attitude towards us but our attitude towards him. The eternal love of God was shown most fully and graphically through his acceptance and forgiveness of the worst that human beings could hurl at him, the killing of his love in the person of his Son Jesus Christ. In this way, the cross did not *bring about* forgiveness – this existed already; but rather, Jesus *enacted* and *represented* the forgiveness which has always been there in the heart of God. His attitude does not change towards us; instead our attitude towards him changes as we see forgiveness acted out before us. The evil we can do is also annihilated in the light of Jesus's resurrection, and we thereby gain confidence to draw near to God in the knowledge that he loves us and is able to transform our lives.

I do not intend to discuss this example any further, other than to say that it gives a taster of how a critical realist approach can work. It may leave some questions: is there, for example, enough of an element of sacrifice to warrant the sacrificial symbolism? Does it exalt love at the cost of righteousness? Will it ultimately matter whether we respond to it or not? But as we have already observed, the legal model begs many questions too. Does God have such changeable emotions? Can he really be placated by the spilling of blood? How does one person's blood being spilt affect the status of billions of other people?

'So, It's Just a Matter of Anything Goes?'

'Aha', somebody says, 'I knew it would come down to this. Now it doesn't matter what you believe, we all just make it up as we go along.' Not at all. Why is it that as soon as we move away from absolutes, we are told that the only option is to float completely free? I would tend to agree with those who see the threat from certainty as greater than that posed by 'anything goes'. There are probably far fewer people who truly believe that anything goes than there are those who think they know for certain what is right. Both extremes are, of course, a deception. I am certainly not advocating an end to objectivity, but I think we must agree with Walter Brueggeman when he says: 'The truth is that there is no answer in the back of the book to which there is assent, no final arbiter who will finally adjudicate rival claims' – not in this life anyway. And as he goes on to say, most of those who want absolutes tend to accept authority only if it makes the absolute claim to which they are already disposed.[13] At this point we only have perspectives on ultimate truth and not ultimate truth itself – the rest is rhetoric.

When people assume that if you do not have absolute truth you are floating free, they are making one very serious value judgment: that you are not seeking absolute truth. In his influential book *Myths, Models and Paradigms*, Ian Barbour speaks of the tension which critical realists must embrace:

- A combination of *faith* and *doubt*.

The 'critical' element recognizes the limitations of religious models. Doubt challenges the dogmatisms and questions the neat schemes in which we think we have truth wrapped up; there is a 'holy insecurity'. Faith is not intellectual certainty or the absence of doubt, but a trust and commitment despite the lack of infallible dogmas. Faith takes us beyond a detached outlook to the sphere of personal involvement.

- A combination of *commitment* and *enquiry*.

Commitment does not rule out critical reflection, continued enquiry and dedication to the search for truth beyond personal preference.

- A combination of *confession* and *self-criticism*.

We can only say that this is what has happened to ourselves and others within our tradition; that this is how things look from where we stand in our paradigm community. Self-criticism arises because we admit that all our formulations of truth are partial and limited, coupled with the conviction that there are criteria by which we can assess our religious beliefs. From this perspective we acknowledge the historical conditioning of every set of conceptual categories and the weakness of every human viewpoint, while also insisting that even one's most fundamental beliefs can be analysed and discussed.[14]

Obviously, much of what we have discussed in this chapter throws into question the way we treat the Bible, so we now need to address this subject more directly.

8 Is the Bible the Word of God?

Our purpose here is straightforward: what is a post-evangelical view of the Bible? I think it is fair to say that post-evangelicals have mixed feelings on the subject. They have an underlying respect for the Bible, and in my experience they are keen to rediscover its relevance to their lives and to their world; yet they also have a backlog of negative feelings about the way they have seen it used in the past. Many of the interpretations they have heard being placed upon it suggest that the Bible stands in opposition to some of the values they hold most dear; and they also struggle with the 'strangeness' of the world it portrays, compared with the reality they confront day by day.

Evangelicals tend to assume routinely that the Bible is the repository of absolute truth and so they do not take kindly to suggestions that its truth may not be as absolute as they imagine. When people begin to question the modern-day relevance of standards or formulations of truth drawn from the Bible, they naturally meet with a barrage of accusations about 'going liberal' or 'playing fast and loose' with God's word. So we need to refocus our vision somewhat and ask whether the Bible should still hold the central place in Christian thinking, and if so, in what way? Is it still to be considered the word of God, or has modern critical insight rendered such claims obsolete?

My underlying concern is to address the issue from the point of view of post-evangelical people who urgently need to find a fresh place for the Bible in their priorities, rather than from the perspective of conservative evangelical critics who are unlikely to agree with much of what I say. Too many people have abandoned Christianity due to wrong and unrealistic expectations which have been instilled in them concerning the Bible; this is why it is crucial for us to find a view of it which both allows us to feel comfortable with its credibility, while also allowing it to speak uncomfortably into our situations, as we might expect from God's word. Much as I would prefer not to begin with a negative, we need to exorcise a ghost which still haunts many people: the claim that the Bible contains no errors, or the doctrine of inerrancy.

Inerrancy – A Monumental Waste of Time!

I have no intention of arguing extensively against this doctrine; I simply marvel that anyone should think it plausible or necessary to believe in such a thing. I will, however, just outline the issues, and state why I think it is an unnecessary burden to carry. As already stated, the issue of inerrancy arises out of the fundamentalist–modernist conflict of the nineteenth and early twentieth centuries. Although its proponents will tell you otherwise, the notion of inerrancy did not exist as such before that, for the simple reason that the questions and criticisms it attempts to answer also did not really exist. It is a rationalist response to a rationalist attack, and it has proved to be one of the most troublesome and divisive pieces of evangelical dogma ever invented. In recent years there have been interminable squabbles between those who favour this or that nuanced version of inerrancy, and I shudder to think how many trees have been felled in the process!

Two of the main weapons of persuasion in the inerrantist armoury are the 'slippery slopes' and the 'all or nothing' gambits. It may sound convincing to a young convert to be told that the entire credibility of the Bible hinges on its being true in every detail, but this is actually a load of tosh. The argument says that if the Bible cannot be trusted on its (fairly incidental) comments on history and science, then it cannot be trusted at all. Francis Schaeffer contended passionately for this position right up to his death. Seeing the issue as a watershed for evangelicals, he called for a line to be drawn 'lovingly, yet clearly' between those who accepted what he called 'the full authority' of Scripture, and those who were opting for the 'slippery slopes' of non-inerrancy. 'Unless the Bible is without error', he wrote, 'not only when it speaks of salvation matters, but also when it speaks of history and the cosmos, we have no foundation for answering questions concerning the existence of the universe . . . nor do we have any moral absolutes, or certainty of salvation.'[1] According to Schaeffer, the Bible is God's word and hence it must be absolutely and objectively true, and not subject to any historical or cultural conditioning. If the Bible says the sun stood still, then it did; if it says that the whole earth was flooded, then it was; and presumably, if it said that Jonah swallowed the whale – well he must have done!

John Stott, on the other hand, is an example of a much more reasonable inerrantist, who distances himself from fundamentalism.[2] He openly says that he dislikes the term inerrancy, preferring to turn the negative into a positive by talking of the 'trustworthiness' of Scripture. He readily sees the need to relativize passages such as those in Job, which contain lengthy accounts of the somewhat questionable discourse of Job's friends; the fact that they are in the Bible, he argues, does not mean that they should be read as God's word. He also recognizes the importance of literary genre, stating that passages which are, for example, clearly poetic should not be judged on scientific grounds. And while still believing that Adam and Eve were actual people, he sees no reason to maintain that the Genesis account of the Creation is a literal statement of how the world began.[3]

It has to be said, however, that Stott is still not really conceding that the Bible contains errors; he is basically applying a better form of biblical interpretation – something which is greatly to be welcomed. But when the chips are down he is an inerrantist, although he qualifies for that position in two ways: firstly, he says that it is only the original autographs (the actual manuscripts produced by the authors) which are inerrant, and secondly, even then, these can only be thought of as inerrant when they are rightly interpreted.[4] Both points are rather academic, since none of the original autographs exists, and in any case who can decide what is a proper interpretation? It does seem strange that God did not ensure that the copying was without error as well as the original writing; we can only assume that he does not mind that most Christians throughout history have had (at best) flawed versions of the Bible, and that they have quite likely interpreted it incorrectly.

In contrast to fundamentalists, and even to many fellow-evangelicals, John Stott offers a much more sensible approach to interpreting the Bible. He also represents a strand of evangelicalism which seeks to deal honestly with modern scholarship, and I believe fewer people would have turned their backs on Christianity had they benefited from his insight and wisdom. Having said that, James Barr probably has a point, when he says,

> Though there may be, and are, many evangelicals . . . who are not fundamentalists, there is little sign that they have, or seek to have a strong and independent position about the Bible, to set against the fundamentalist one . . . under strain and pressure from critics they will try to display a more open position, but left to themselves, they will fall back on a fundamentalist position, modified as little as possible.[5]

I need not use space here to point out typical problems and discrepancies in the Bible; many others have done a convincing enough job of this.[6] Suffice it to say that anyone with even a modicum of critical perception can see, for example, the inconsistencies between the Gospel accounts. Endless attempts are made to 'harmonize' such discrepancies and to make out that no problem exists, but frankly, many of these exercises stretch one's credulity to breaking point. For instance, an elaborate reconstruction of the cock-crowing incident surrounding Peter's denial attempts to harmonize the obvious (though inconsequential) differences between the Gospel accounts as to how many denials actually took place and how many times the cock crowed. The proposed 'solution' constructs an event

based on all four accounts, in which each of them represents only a partial view. The outcome is not a threefold, but a sixfold denial by Peter, with three denials
preceding the first crowing, and a further three preceding the second crowing. Apart from the obvious question as to why anyone would bother to go to all this
trouble, the reconstructed version actually lands up in
a position where *none* of the Gospels gives an objectively true picture of what happened![7]

Arguably the most important reason why inerrancy
is a monumental waste of time is that the Bible clearly
does not claim it for itself. Indeed, the Bible has
remarkably little to say about itself or the nature of its
divine sources: 'One gets the impression that its chief
task is to point away from itself to something or someone who is far more important.'[8] There are certainly
passages which affirm its divine inspiration (2 Timothy
3.16 and 2 Peter 1.20–1), but none of them suggests or
implies inerrancy. Inerrancy is an ideology introduced
into the text from outside. James Barr, who has written
extensively on the subject, argues forcefully that inerrancy is a (believing) rationalist response to (an unbelieving) rationalist threat. It is rationalist, he says, in
that it is based on the reasoning that Scripture cannot
be inspired unless it is historically inerrant.[9] Such a
limited notion of inspiration is clearly linked more to
the 'scientific' type of language, mentioned in the last
chapter, than to the 'poetic' type of language.

The Bible as Word of God – In What Sense?

The inerrantist argument is that the Bible can be the
word of God only if it is entirely without error. So if we

accept that the Bible does contain errors, mistakes and discrepancies, in what sense can it continue to be the word of God? Is it not best simply to conclude that it is an interesting ancient text, which gives us a record of the background to Christianity and the way early Christians interpreted their faith? I do not think so, and fortunately I am not alone in recognizing that the Bible can be both a human book, with all the consequent limitations, and a contemporary medium for divine revelation. To get a framework in which the Bible can be seen as the word of God, we will begin by looking at the theology of Karl Barth, who has been described as the first truly postmodern theologian.

Barth has brought us the most sophisticated understanding of the term 'word of God'. Moving right away from the territory of the inerrancy debate, he saw revelation as primarily personal and not verbal; revelation is about the self-disclosure of God rather than a set of verbal propositions about him, whether errant or inerrant. The word of God, according to Barth, has a threefold form: the primary form is the *living Word* expressed in Jesus Christ; the secondary form is the *written word* of Scripture, which testifies to the living Word; and the third form is the *proclaimed word* which is the church's proclamation of Christ the living Word. The three are inextricably linked together, the Word of God in Christ being primary. The Bible, therefore, according to Barth, is not in itself revelation; instead it testifies to the revelation of God in Christ. 'No one who reads the Bible carefully', he says, 'will find in it any claim that its texts are, as such, a revelation of God.' On the other hand, he continues, it is equally wrong to say (like the liberals) that the Bible merely includes the revelation of God: the whole of the Bible, he insists, is 'pregnant with revelation'. In itself, however, it is only a collection of human documents which people have written in the language of human beings, at a definite time and in a definite situation; consequently, any search for an absolute and unconditional source of divine revelation, Barth believed, inevitably came up against the limitations of the biblical authors and the relativity of their time and culture.

Another associated idea of Barth's is the view that the Bible has two dimensions, one human and one divine. Just as Christ is held to be truly God and truly man, so the Bible is both word of God and word of man. This does not imply that some parts are human and other parts are divine, any more than some parts of Christ were human and others divine. The entire Bible is human word, subject to the strains, weaknesses and errors of any human product, and therefore requires to be examined and studied with all the critical methods available. Yet it is also divine word, in that it has something to say which does not arise out of human cogitations or human culture, and therefore it must also be studied with a listening ear, to hear what God will say through it.

Barth also spoke of the Bible *becoming*, rather than *being*, the word of God. It is perfectly possible to read it, and indeed to study it in a scholarly way, and only ever bump into the imperfect human dimension (just as one might have only encountered the humanity of Jesus) and never hear God speaking through it. The word of God in that sense is not a static quality of the Bible, but something which comes into being as God speaks through it in a living and dynamic way. This is what

Barth meant by saying that the Bible is pregnant with revelation.[10]

While offering an excellent framework in which to view Scripture as the word of God, Barth's approach raises some other questions. For instance, is the Christian narrative the only way in which God has revealed himself? Are there other witnesses to the living Word apart from Scripture, or other means by which Christ is communicated apart from preaching and teaching? Since we are primarily concerned here with looking at how the Bible in particular speaks God's word, we will settle for just flagging up these questions for the moment.

How Does the Bible Speak God's Word?

Having got a framework in which to see the Bible as truly the word of God, while still fully accommodating its human limitations, we now need to ask *how* it speaks God's word and what the nature of divine revelation is. Sandra Schneiders, a Catholic theologian, offers some invaluable insights which accord with the critical realist approach to truth already described in the last chapter.[11]

'WORD OF GOD' – A METAPHOR

To talk about Scripture as the word of God is actually to employ a metaphor; God cannot be thought of as literally speaking words, since they are an entirely human phenomenon which could never prove adequate as a medium for the speech of an infinite God, even if he did speak in a literal way. Just as we do not think of God having physical eyes in order to 'read' our

112

thoughts or an actual 'arm' with which to deliver his people, so we should not think of God as literally speaking words.

Sadly, the only alternative in many people's minds to a literal understanding of the phrase 'word of God' is to interpret it as being fanciful and untrue. But as we saw in the previous chapter, this is to miss the whole point of metaphoric language, which is deliberately paradoxical, having at its heart an unresolvable tension – an 'is/is not' (God is/is not our father). To treat 'word of God' as a mere figure of speech is to 'resolve' that tension, kill the metaphor and reduce the phrase to a synonym for the Bible, which is then rendered a mere religious book. To take the phrase literally is to suggest that the Bible actually constitutes a document of divine speech, in which human language is attributed to God. Commenting that literalism is the 'cancer of the re-ligious imagination', Schneiders says that people who pursue it

> must regard each and every word of the Scriptures as equally and fully divine and thus absolutely true . . . . The impasses to which this leads, the ab-surdity of the truth claims that must be made for patent human errors in the text, are too well known to require repetition.[12]

Describing the phrase 'word of God' as a metaphor, then, in itself does not detract from its truth. The cru-cial question is, to what does the 'is' of the metaphor refer? We know in what way the Bible 'is not' the word of God – it is a book of human documents – but in what way 'is' it the word of God? We can affirm that it is the word of God in that it is the symbolic location of divine revelation: people have found it to be a place where they encounter God and understand something of his truth. But in what way does it reveal God and his truth if not through verbal propositions?

'WORD OF GOD' – A SYMBOLIC REVELATION

The answer to this question is that God does reveal himself through verbal propositions, through words and sentences, through semantics and syntax, but in a symbolic rather than a literal way. The fact that we have a Bible filled with propositions, and the fact that we legitimately continue to struggle to formulate words which express divine truth, whether in creeds, in systematic theology, or in sermons, should not fool us into thinking that these words are in and of themselves that truth. They are symbols of truth. We can and should study them, analyse them, meditate upon them and absorb them, but we must not imagine that they *are* the truth.

It might help at this point if we say what we mean by a symbol. Schneiders gives four helpful pointers.

- A symbol is not a sign or an indicator of something other than itself, like a motorway sign which points to a place several miles away, nor is it a stand-in or a substitute for something which is not really there. A symbol is a vehicle of the presence of something or someone that cannot be encountered in any other way. Whether a symbol is a physical entity or a mental image, its essential job is to make something perceptible which is otherwise imperceptible.
- A symbol does not symbolize in a vacuum, but only in interaction with the person who engages with it.

In itself it remains lifeless, but once someone engages with it, it becomes active and can deliver its meaning – its revelatory powers are unleashed.

- Unlike a sign, which is a separate entity standing for something other than itself, a symbol participates directly in the presence and power of that which it symbolizes. Rather than being something which has to be bypassed or overcome, it mediates the thing or person which it symbolizes.

- Paradoxically, a symbol brings to expression something which it cannot fully express. Schneiders likens it to a pinpoint of starlight in a vast and otherwise darkened sky. In that background lies an unfathomable network of stars and planetary systems which remain unseen. Since the symbol is but a minuscule manifestation of a vast background of 'unsaid', it must always remain ambiguous and allusive, concealing, in fact, more than it reveals.[13]

Bear in mind that revelation is not primarily about imparting facts, but the disclosure of a person; it is the 'divine self-gift which has been taking place from the moment of creation and will continue to the end of time'.[14] Whilst this divine 'self-giving' reached its zenith in the Christ-event, God has been pleased also to reveal himself through the testimony to that event throughout the whole of Scripture. Through the complex symbolism of its narrative, its pictures and images, its parables and legends, its metaphors and analogies and its plain statements, the presence of God is mediated powerfully and intelligently. Being symbolic, however, the truth must be understood as ambiguous and in need of constant reinterpretation.

The philosopher Martin Heidegger spoke of language as a 'house of being', the place where inner being comes into the open through self-disclosure. Put more simply, we do not primarily speak to impart information but as a means of self-expression; and we do not really understand language – we understand *through* language.[15] To grasp the way in which Scripture reveals God's word, we must learn to appreciate the symbolic rather than the purely mechanical or technical nature of human language. As I have said, this in no way makes the words and grammar unimportant – far from it – but it emphasizes that our primary attention, and our faith-response to the Bible, is not to the words, but to the One who is being sacramentally revealed through the words.

How do we Hear God's Word?

The notion that everything can be reduced to an exact statement of words is a distinctly Enlightenment perspective, based on a subject–object relationship. Both liberals and evangelicals have tended, for different reasons, to fall into the same trap of objectifying Scripture. The liberals have done it because they believe that the texts are only texts, and hence they are simply words which can be the subject of intellectual criticism; many evangelicals have objectified the text because they believe that the words are literally God's words and so require detailed analysis. Understanding the word of God as symbolic revelation, however, leads the interpreter away from a subject–object relationship into a more intuitive involvement with the revelatory process.

We have already noted, however, that Scripture does not automatically become the living and dynamic word of God to the reader or listener; the Bible may remain a mere book of human words and stories, pregnant with revelation yet never giving birth. To say that this is simply a case of 'beauty in the eye of the beholder' reduces the matter of revelation to the level of aesthetics, which is unsatisfactory for the believer. Our ability to examine how the word of God is actualized is obviously limited to the human perspective, and I will attempt to comment on this using three key words: faith, imagination and brains.

'TAKE IT ON FAITH'

It is commonly believed that faith is a pretty unscientific state of affairs, 'an ungrounded persuasion' of the mind, as Locke put it. Michael Polanyi, a scientist whose thinking on the theory of knowledge has proved highly influential, denies this assumption completely. In line with Isaiah's statement that 'If you will not believe, you will not understand' (Isaiah 7.9)[16], Polanyi has insisted that all knowing is fiduciary, that is to say, based on a measure of trust or faith. Flying full in the face of Enlightenment objectivism he said that we cannot know things from the outside; in order to know something we must 'indwell' it: 'we cease to handle things and become immersed in them.'[17] What this means is that we must always begin with a faith-commitment, hence presuppositions are not to be seen as enemies of honest research but as basic essentials. But this faith element is not, in Polanyi's judgment, a matter of cold choice; it arises out of a kind of intuitive compulsion – call it a hunch – which provides the impetus for faith.

There are also two vitally related aspects of scientific belief which Polanyi noted. The first is that when we adopt one way of looking at things, we automatically exclude other ways of looking at them; faith has a necessary exclusiveness about it. But if something is conceivable, it is also conceivably wrong; consequently, the second essential to such faith is the need to be equally resolute in testing our faith-commitments with rigorous self-criticism in order to distinguish between ultimate beliefs and subjective notions.[18] These two points teach us something very fundamental about faith: that there is a dialectical tension at the very heart of faith between *commitment* and *doubt*. There is no inherent contradiction between faith and reason provided this tension is maintained.

It seems to me that far too often the initial 'hunch' which leads people to believe in Christ, and to discover his revelation through Scripture, later turns into presumption and a sense of certainty which actually works against the further growth of faith. I believe the reason for this is that the tension between commitment and doubt has subsided or has been completely abandoned. To return to the subject, then, we can say that it is futile to try to prove the divine presence mediated through Scripture by some objective means. The only way we know it is by the 'indwelling' of a faith-commitment, which needs to be held in continuous tension with a process of doubt and self-criticism. To lose the faith-commitment is to handle a mere book; to abandon the critical process, is to commit intellectual suicide.

'USE YOUR IMAGINATION'
Imagination is essential in hearing God's word for two reasons. The first arises out of our assertion that

revelation is essentially symbolic in nature. Symbols operate at an intuitive, rather than a purely rational level, and imagination is the medium for intuition. The second reason is closely linked with this, which is that faith also operates at an intuitive and an imaginative level. Polanyi, building on the revolutionary work of Einstein, removed the stigma from imagination and intuition (which continued to be present in much popular science), and restored their credibility as true sources of knowledge. Imagination is, after all, the quintessential human act, which can challenge all our settled certitudes. Brueggeman describes it as the human capacity to picture, portray, receive and practise the world in ways other than it appears to be at first glance, when seen through a dominant, unexamined lens.[19] In other words, imagination is that ability to see the world 'as' it might be rather than as it is. Imagination is the seed-bed of transformation, and Scripture can become the treasure trove of God's word, out of which it can be funded. Of the countless ways in which the imagination can and does mediate the word of God through Scripture, I can only mention a few.

Meditation. This is a form of mental reflection in which the mind moves back and forth through a particular passage, narrative or character. Walter Wink[20] has provided an especially useful form of meditation which combines Ignatian meditation with insights and techniques from psychotherapy. I have successfully used this with groups in which, for example, we have spent time thinking about the characters in the parable of the prodigal son. As folk have imaginatively 'indwelt' the characters it has been fascinating to see the personal insights which have emerged, and the transforming effects which can follow.

Contemplation. In contrast contemplation seeks to get away from reflective focus and fresh mental insights. What is sought here is a way of expressing deep inner emotions of thankfulness, love or trust towards God in a kind of mystic communion. Scripture might be used here in a repetitive symbolic fashion, in which the meaning of the words subsides into a great sense of wholeness with the One who lies beyond them. Contemplation has the effect of detaching us from the automatic function of the mind which limits our perception, and rhythm is a way of prolonging that moment of contemplation. Taizé music with rhythmic repetitions of Scripture verses have proved very powerful in this respect. If it is to remain Christian, contemplation needs to be funded by the great images and symbols of the Christian narrative. It can quite often be used as an extension of meditation.

Recitation and Story-telling. Hans-Ruedi Weber,[21] who has developed excellent imaginative exercises in the use of Scripture, says that even where oral testimonies were written down, they were not in the first place intended for silent reading; they were meant to be read aloud. The fact that we have a high level of literacy should not rob us of the enormous benefits of just reading Scripture aloud. The skills of reading and telling stories have been swallowed up in the more directive and less allusive craft of rhetoric. We need to rediscover them.

Art Therapy/Bible Meditation. Imagination is a way of breaking with words while still interacting with them. You may have done drawings of Bible stories at Sunday School or the like, but have you tried anything similar as an adult? Using the methods and insights of (non-directive) art therapy, all kinds of things can begin to happen when we learn to portray the feelings and ideas emerging out of the symbolism of Scripture.

Bible Study. Our approach to studying the Bible needs to move away from the very directive style of an 'expert' teaching the novice towards a more communal experience which heightens the imaginative process. In no way am I detracting from the importance of scholarship and learning, but we need to find ways of this being used as a resource for the communal exercise rather than as a didactic oracle. Obviously, books and reference material can be used in this way, but it is even better if we can draw on a 'live' resource person. This sort of communal study almost inevitably has the effect of making people want more.

Theological Study. This might be no more than an intellectual exercise, and yet the word of God can be imaginatively brought to life even in the midst of academic enterprise. C.S. Lewis spoke scathingly of much devotional study of Scripture, which he saw as frequently awash in sentimentalism. He spoke of loving nothing more than to be puzzling over a tough theological issue with a pencil in his hand and a pipe between his teeth: to be highly recommended.

In his excellent book *Experiments with Bible Study* Hans-Ruedi Weber has developed a whole battery of methods of imaginative study of Scripture. Much of the stimulus for his work arose out of being given the challenge in 1953 of bringing basic Christian instruction to a largely illiterate community of believers in a remote part of Indonesia. Having overcome his initial Western response of 'we must teach them to read and write', a wonderful experiment followed. The results, in terms of his 'laboratory' approach to diverse forms of imaginative study, are tremendous, and include everything from drama to story-telling, from clay modelling to role-play, and from drawing to memory games.

To sum up, we can say that it is perfectly legitimate to describe the Bible as God's word provided we recognize that the 'word' is an event mediated by the Bible and not the book itself. Because of the dual nature of Scripture, both human and divine, we need to approach it with all the critical skills available, while also bringing to it qualities of faith and imagination through which we can expect to find God revealing himself. If post-evangelicals fail to achieve this composite response, they will either slip back into the sense of certainty which so often dogs evangelicals, or into the chilly wastes of liberal objectivism, or, worse still, into ex-Christianity.

9 Positively Worldly

> This world is not my home,
> I'm just a-passing through;
> My treasures are laid up
> Somewhere beyond the blue
> The Saviour beckons me
> From heaven's open door,
> And I can't feel at home
> In this world any more.[1]

This song was the anthem of my early Christian experience. With its rough and ready sentimentalism it summed up so much of the theology and piety of my particular church background, where it was considered that the only people who felt at home in this world were the unconverted and backsliders. The world, so I was told, was enemy territory, a place full of temptations and pitfalls for the Christian. We had no choice but to venture out into the world on a day-to-day basis, but the clear policy was 'avoidance wherever possible'. Don't put yourself in situations of temptation, I was urged; avoid places like cinemas, theatres, clubs and pubs; avoid friendships with unbelievers (especially unbelieving girlfriends) unless it is for evangelistic purposes, and avoid filling your head with 'worldly' thoughts and passions. The rule of thumb was: 'if you want it, it's probably wrong'! I remember feeling guilty about my lurking desires to stay in this

world for a while and enjoy some of its pleasures before advancing to the goody-goody pleasures of the
world beyond. Of course, I would never have admitted
it.

The Parallel Universe

Things have loosened up since then, and standards
have changed; nowadays, not too many eyebrows are
raised about someone going to the cinema or the theatre (depending perhaps on what is showing); reading
the Sunday papers is no longer a sin, and teetotalism is
no longer mandatory. Yet the underlying distrust of the
world is still evident, and fear of contamination is
never far away. The solution now, however, lies less in
legalistic prohibitions and more in generating christianized alternatives to the world. Indeed, the Christian
sub-culture has never known such a boom period in
which 'disinfected' versions of previously forbidden
fruit abound. It is like a parallel universe: Christian
festivals, Christian records, Christian holidays, Christian social events, Christian dating agencies, Christian
theatre, Christian comedy, Christian television, Christian aerobics set to Christian music – it seems like the
resourcefulness of 'Christian' imitation knows no
bounds. I even saw an advertisement in a Christian
magazine this week for Christian computer games.
'Sick of Virtual Mayhem?', it read. 'At last a Christian
alternative.' Yes: Christian software is here, with
games like 'Spiritual Warfare' (the UK's top seller, we
are assured). I guess we will progress to 'Mario gets
saved', 'Church Plant in Sin City' or 'Virtual Millen-
nium'. Of course, we already have Christian science-

fiction books like Frank Perretti's *This Present Darkness* and *Piercing the Darkness*.

Not that Christian alternativism consists purely of entertainment substitutes; there is a surge of interest in serious Christian social involvement initiatives, with a plethora of relevant organizations and projects emerging. Christian education is also a matter of great concern, with church schools appearing all over the place. There are Christian businesses, law practices, medical centres and so on. I do not doubt that many of these initiatives serve a real purpose and help meet vital needs, but I cannot help wondering what lies behind this whole strategy of Christian alternativism. Why does everything have to have a 'Christian' label? Why do we not simply lend our support to the perfectly effective so-called 'secular' versions which already exist? Does it not betray a basic antipathy towards the world?

Few topics are more important to post-evangelicals than the Christian's relationship with the world. The 'parallel universe' of alternativism constitutes a substantial part of what they wish to leave behind. For them, feeling at home in this world is not all bad, and indeed they will freely confess that they often find non-Christian friendships more satisfying than friendships with fellow-Christians. As one person told me, 'I feel I am supposed to have things in common with Christians, and generally I can't say I do; whereas with non-Christians I feel there are fewer expectations in the relationship.' Post-evangelicals also look at culture more positively and testify to feeling more stimulation – even spiritual stimulation – from 'secular' sources than they do from sources within the evangelical sub-culture. Clearly there are major issues at stake, and potential hazards on all sides, so we need to explore one or two principle themes. We shall begin on the very fundamental level of how we understand the human condition from a theological perspective.

'Man . . . A Bundle of Contradictions'

'Man is an embodied paradox, a bundle of contradictions.'[2] This succinct comment on the human situation resonates well with the narrative and symbolism surrounding the Genesis account of human origins. The *paradox* of the human condition is exquisitely symbolized by the dual factors in the creative process: that on the one hand Adam was formed from the dust of the earth, and that on the other he was made alive by the breath of God. Apart from anything else, this dual source of human life has profound ecological implications. Human beings are both *a part of*, and *apart from* the rest of their environment. The 'apart from' factor is what upsets conservationists and for good reason; the notion of human superiority has proved to be the ideological basis for the wholesale abuse and destruction of nature. Biblically, however, the task of stewardship (for that is how 'take dominion' must be interpreted) is intrinsically linked to the divine initiative to 'make human beings in our image' (Genesis 1.26, Revised English Bible). In other words, the human mandate amounts to nothing more or less than a commission to represent the Creator and Preserver of the world – to be his 'justice of the peace' in the earthly situation.[3]

The *contradictions* in the human condition lie in the fact that the image of God, which humanity still bears, has been corrupted through sin. The degree to which that image is, or is not, still present, both within the individual and within the collective human experience, is crucial to our subject, since our understanding of the world hinges on our understanding of the individual human condition.

Speculation abounds as to what it means that human beings were made in God's image. It is commonly thought that the *imago Dei* consisted of certain residual qualities in us, such as rationality, will or responsibility, or, more importantly, the possession of a soul, which it has always been assumed is a characteristic unique to humans (although the status of animals is now being rethought).[4] Personally, I prefer a more existential explanation such as that given by John Macquarrie, who argues that the *imago Dei* is best understood in terms of the human capacity for 'being'. Unlike any other creature, human beings experience an openness in which they can move outward and upward.[5] In other words humans have the potentiality to actualize themselves in relationship to other beings, and indeed to divine Being, to grow spiritually, morally and intellectually. The *imago Dei* is therefore not conceived as a fixed 'nature', but as a capacity to 'be' God-like.

We know from theology and experience, however, that this capacity to be God-like has been crippled through sin, but how much is it crippled and what are the implications? John Calvin took one of the gloomier views of this subject in his discussion of what he called the 'total depravity of man'. In his view, the image of God was effaced by sin, and man was incapable of any good other than that which resulted from the divine 'restraining grace'. 'Everything proceeding from the corrupt nature is damnable', he said; and any apparent manifestations of 'good nature' or virtue in unregenerate people is illusory and worthless.[6]

I am certainly not alone in seeing this assessment as both unbiblical and profoundly unhelpful. So how can we restate the meaning and effects of the Fall on the human situation? First, we must acknowledge that the condition of sinfulness in human beings is self-inflicted. If Genesis teaches us anything, it is that sin entered the scene through a blatant disregard for what God said. Second, we can identify the basic essence of sin as idolatry. In existential language, it was a turning from Being to beings, the effort of man to found life on himself, to give life meaning in terms of the finite, to the exclusion of the Infinite. This idolatry should not be seen simply as a mistaken belief, but as a perverse faith commitment: an act of the will.[7] Third, human fallenness is universal: every part of every person is affected; its horizons are limitless. And fourth, man is incapable of reversing its effects without the presence of divine grace.

Having said all of this, we must swiftly add a couple of riders. We should first add that the image of God in humanity, though defaced, is not effaced; although every part of every person is affected by the Fall, they are not all affected as much as they could be. Common observation confirms this: one does not have to be a Christian to be good, moral, loving, dedicated, creative, sacrificing, joyful, and so on. Remember the fourth point above: none of these qualities are, in themselves, redemptive of the human situation, but they are, nevertheless, manifestations of God-likeness.

This brings us to a second rider, which is that while it is true that human beings cannot reverse their situation, or in any way create their own redemption, the very helplessness of their position evokes a search for the grace which alone can solve their predicament. Or as Macquarrie so aptly puts it, 'If there is original sin, there is also original righteousness, if only in the form of longing for release and for fullness of existence.'[8]

I would be surprised if these comments create too much difficulty for most evangelicals, but there may well be a significant difference of emphasis. As a generalization, evangelicals tend to give the nod to the point about God's image being still present in man, but when it comes to unbelievers, their emphasis is almost entirely on their fallenness. This is not an insignificant item: it has a major bearing on the Christian's posture towards the world and a significant effect on the evangelistic situation. An example of what I mean can be seen when we ask how a Christian differs from a non-Christian.

The question is, of course, too general; the differences between particular people may be immense, and some of this may be directly attributable to the faith of the one person, and some of it might be due to other factors altogether. The level at which I am pitching the question relates to what we might call the inner pilgrimage, and not to the matter of intellectual knowledge. If we accept that the quest for grace which I mentioned earlier may be taking place long before someone believes or even considers believing in Christ; and if we accept that God grants his grace to those who seek, even though they know not what they seek, then the whole situation is far more complex than a crude

Christian–non-Christian analysis might suggest. There is surely a significant difference between the *knowledge* and the *presence* of God's grace. Some may have knowledge yet have little existential presence of grace, while others may have little knowledge of it yet a great deal of its existential presence.

C.S. Lewis makes a very similar point when he talks about heaven and hell as ways or 'being', rather than as geographical locations. Instead of focusing on one particular decision as determinitive of a person's destiny, Lewis portrays life as a long series of decisions or choices of being – choices of whether to be this or that sort of person. 'Each of us, at each moment, is progressing to the one state or the other.'[9] Adopting such a perspective significantly affects the way we relate to the world around us. Rather than looking at things territorially – the church as God's (therefore safe) territory, and the world as the devil's (therefore dangerous) territory – or dealing with rigid categories ('church', 'world', 'Christian', 'non-Christian', etc.) we envisage God at work in his world, revealing himself in all kinds of ways and responding to the inner yearnings and the faith-commitments of people everywhere. The world then ceases to be clearcut, and we find ourselves dealing not only with the 'bundle of contradictions' in the human situation, but also with the eternal Being who is poured out.

A World of Difference

This leads us to the practical question of how we should relate to the world, by which I mean people and culture. So far we have recognized the ambivalence of the human condition: that it reflects something of the image of God and at the same time something of the corruption of the Fall. As we move on from the individual to the question of culture, I shall argue that the same basic characteristic is also true of culture: it too bears both the imprint of God and the corruption of human sinfulness. But first we need to define what we mean by culture.

'Culture' is an infamously slippery term. A widely accepted definition states that 'The culture of a society is the way of life of its members; the collection of ideas and habits which they learn, share and transmit from generation to generation.'[10] We only become aware of our immense amount of cultural baggage when we spend time in a different culture. It is then that we begin to realize that we are inextricably bound to our culture. It is in the way we think, the way we speak. Translating a phrase like 'Sunday lunch' may be quite easy on a purely word-for-word basis, but infinitely more will be left unsaid by way of cultural nuances, expectations and memories than will ever be communicated. Without a shared culture the members of a society would be unable to communicate and co-operate, or even know how to identify themselves, for to a large degree culture determines how we think and feel; it directs our actions and defines our outlook on life.[11] What I am saying is simply this: we cannot and do not 'exist' without a cultural identity.

To take it one step further, we can say that our entire concept of God is conditioned by culture, both by that of other cultures of previous generations and by our own. This is inevitable, since the only way we have of conceptualizing or envisaging God is through language, and language is cultural. Indeed the whole theological enterprise is, of necessity, a cultural exercise. If theology is to make any sense, it must use the language of its surrounding culture, and this in turn affects what theology is saying. And it follows, therefore, that no theology can be final; it has to be formulated and reformulated, over and over, as cultural conditions change. We simply cannot escape culture any more than we can escape language: language and culture are us, just as we are them. I need not go over the argument I have already set out, that this provisional nature of truth in no way denies that there is such a thing as objective truth and reality, it simply emphasizes our own inability to verbalize it or 'possess' it. In this sense I like to think of truth as I think of a person whom I deeply desire to know. The more my knowledge of that person increases, the more I realize that absolute knowledge of him or her will forever escape me. For to have such knowledge would be to 'possess' the person and this I cannot do. Indeed, if such knowledge were possible, it would probably mean the death of the relationship, for the quest would be over.

Since culture is an extension of the human being, it follows that it reflects both the 'paradox' and the 'bundle of contradictions' which we have already discussed: the glorious paradox of the earthy and the transcendent, and the awful contradiction of the divine and the sinful. All these factors are inescapably present in human culture. It follows, therefore, that to categorize something like a record, a painting, a novel or a system of education as 'Christian' or 'non-Christian' (or more commonly 'secular') is quite often to judge such things only on their superficial merits – for example, whether or not they talk explicitly about Christian themes. In reality, there will almost always be a mixture of influences, and discerning which is a dominant influence does not mean looking at the obvious signs. For instance, a song may well be recorded by Christians and have lyrics with an overtly Christian theme, yet it can nevertheless betray attitudes like arrogance, intolerance or sexism which are profoundly unchristian. On the other hand, a so-called secular album may, on the surface, be criticizing or even ridiculing Christianity, and yet at the same time be conveying a deeply Christian truth.

The Fingerprints of God

It is quite common to hear post-evangelicals (as well as many staunch evangelicals) bemoaning the quality of cultural life in the church: 'Christians always produce second-rate versions of what the secular world does very well', someone said to me recently. But it would be wrong to imagine that this is just a matter of taste. Very often, secular artists, writers or performers are actually wrestling with issues or celebrating life in deeper and more evocative ways than their Christian counterparts. Consequently, films, plays, books, music, dance or even soap operas can often provide significant insights, moral questionings, or reflections on human relationships which stimulate one's spiritual life in a way that hardly ever happens in the Christian ghetto.

One significant factor which frequently causes secular culture to be more evocative and stimulating is the greater freedom among non-Christians to explore the full gamut of human emotion. Evangelicals in particular suffer from a compulsion to associate their faith with euphoric and joyful feelings, with little or no acknowledgement of darker emotions. An unfortunate spin-off of this is that people suffering from depression are made to feel a sense of guilt and condemnation. But there is more to it than this; an enormous amount of creativity stems from the darker side of human experience, and yet this creativity tends to be stifled under a relentless tide of joyfulness and triumphalism. And then of course, there are sexual and erotic feelings which are not really explored; there is humorous innuendo and so much more which is treated as forbidden territory.

One of my pleasures over the years, as I have aired these topics through the medium of public talks and sermons, has been to find myself welcomed by relieved people, who had given up hope that their love of theatre, films, or comedy would ever be affirmed as an integral part of their Christian experience. And they are not all young people; I remember a widow in her mid-sixties who said, 'You don't know what a burden you have lifted from me tonight. I have enjoyed reading novels and going to the theatre for years, and I have become weary of people chiding me and telling me to do something more edifying with my time.'

Some of us have tried to turn the issue around and introduce some of the 'worldly' stimulation back into the church; it has not been easy. When we decided to organize an arts festival called 'HARRY' (because it took place at the Harrogate Showground) we thought long and hard about these things. Our dilemma was that we wanted to have an event at which we, the organizers, did not have to apologize for our faith and yet which did not function as a 'Christian' event. We decided to include artists and speakers who did not necessarily share our faith but who could contribute qualitatively to the event, and we aimed to attract an audience which cut across the Christian/non-Christian divide. In many ways it has been a modest venture, which has failed to go as far as we wished, yet the most remarkable thing has been the negative response from Christians, especially from church leaders. 'Was that band Christian?' 'Did you know that rainbows are a symbol of the New Age?' 'Was that speaker evangelical?' 'How many people got saved?' were just a few of the many bemusing questions we have faced. Thankfully there is another side as well: non-believing artists, speakers and punters who have repeatedly said that this was the kind of Christianity they could relate to; churchgoing people who said, 'It's not like a Christian event – it's great'; and artists who are Christians saying that they felt they had come home at last.

Of course, there are conspicuous pitfalls for those who are resolved to be 'positively worldly'. As we have recognized, the world, like the individual, is ambivalent – 'a bundle of contradictions'. There is much around us which is antagonistic to God and to the spirit of Christianity, and so we cannot just swallow whatever is presented to us. Many think this is exactly what liberalism has done. In his apologetic for liberal Christianity Donald Miller acknowledges the temptation: 'The danger in liberalism is that its Christian message may become a mirror reflection of the spirit of the age. This is an ever-present problem for liberal Christians to confront . . . . It is in losing the tension between Christ and culture that liberal Christianity has frequently lost its soul.'[12] Yet

Miller has a strong point when he argues that one cannot possibly criticize a culture without understanding it, and this is precisely where so much of evangelicalism has fallen down: it has failed to engage positively with the surrounding culture.

The relevance to the post-evangelical situation of Miller's sound assessment of the liberal pitfalls cannot be over-emphasized. We have to find a way of engaging positively with our culture without giving in to its anti-Christian influences. I will finish this chapter with a few pointers, which might prove helpful as we follow this path of positive engagement.

To begin with, we need much more opportunity for *communal reflection* on issues raised by contemporary culture. On the whole, the church does not provide this; the best we generally get are rather negative and ill-informed comments from the pulpit. Forums such as our own at Holy Joe's, where we enjoy open discussion or debate on such issues, could easily be produced in a variety of different settings; it is easy to organize an informal group in someone's home or down at the pub. I will offer just a couple of guidelines. You will find it very helpful to put a bit of structure into the discussion: do not just breeze into themes but decide on them beforehand. Appoint an informal chairperson, who can ensure fair play, and keep the discussion on track. And avoid the temptation to formulate a Christian 'line' on issues; do not be afraid of open-ended conclusions.

Then, both on the communal and the individual level, we need to make continual use of the *biblical text* as the arena for thinking about and discussing the issues raised. The method of trying to apply the Bible in textbook style to contemporary issues leads either to absurd, literalistic legalism or to a dead end of frustration, born out of the fact that the text just does not work when used in that way. The alternative is to allow Scripture to *fund* our deliberations, or to act as a lens through which we view the contemporary world. At times the text seems hopelessly remote from the real world with which we have to do, and the temptation is to stop wrestling with it, choosing instead to rely simply on our natural reactions or our mental deliberations: this is a serious mistake.

The best place to pursue this point is in a group. Very often you find that some people tackle issues on a purely pragmatic level, while others tend to think along biblical lines; both elements are necessary and they can balance one another. The Bible seldom provides direct comment on contemporary cultural issues, but by grappling with such issues in the matrix of what Barth called 'the strange world' of the Bible, we can find God's word emerging in a highly relevant fashion.

Lastly, we must take all care to maintain *uncompromised integrity*. The conscience is a flawed and fallible piece of apparatus, which is inevitably in a state of constant readjustment, but it is important that we do not flout it carelessly. When Paul speaks about the different standards of his fellow-Christians (for example choosing to eat or not eat meat or things offered to idols) he makes the comment that 'whatever is not of faith is sin' (Romans 14.23), by which he means that it is probably more important that we are true to our convictions than whether our convictions ultimately prove to be correct or not. We must not do things simply because others do them, nor force others to do things simply because we are happy about them.

Wherever we turn in God's world we find his finger-prints, not just in the glories of the countryside but also in the tangled web of human life and culture. With all the contradictions and ambiguities we encounter and experience in the world, we must never allow ourselves to forget that God is in the world, laughing, singing, shouting, whispering, healing, weeping, reconciling, enabling, resisting, forgiving . . . . He has not given up on it and neither should we. I have long admired the writings of Michel Quoist, and especially his little classic *Prayers of Life*,[13] which envisages a God involved with telephones, roller-skates, glasses of beer, tractors, football matches and delinquents. When he visited the HARRY Festival a couple of years ago, smoking his pipe and charming audiences with his French accent and his twinkling eyes, someone asked me, 'How come a 72 year-old lifelong celibate priest knows so much about life: about love, relationships, sexuality, and enjoying life?' The answer? He's positively worldly!

10 Christianity for a New Age

A friend of mine recently asked a well known evangelical leader if he had heard of the term 'post-evangelical'. 'Post-evangelical?' the man replied, 'Post-evangelical? Whatever is a post-evangelical? Surely, my boy, one either is an evangelical, or one is not an evangelical. Which is it?' The plain fact of the matter is, though, that an increasing number of people see themselves as post-evangelical and many others identify with what being post-evangelical means, without actually using the term. Something is happening which is infinitely more significant than whether or not a bunch of evangelical 'drop outs' can find a constructive way forward. My thesis has been that this bigger something is linked to a fundamental cultural shift which is taking place in the Western world: a shift from the modern to the postmodern.

The challenge to churches of all traditions is how to adjust to the changes which are taking place, and how to express eternal truth in and through this emerging culture. It seems to me that there is a basic separation from those who see the only solution to be that of returning (in some cases with a vengeance) to the older certainties; in effect these people are saying that the only response to a sea of uncertainty is to re-establish the presence of absolute certainty. This approach is understandable, and it is clear that there is a considerable 'market' for it. After all, it offers a sense of security and familiarity in the midst of a lot of confusion. But for lots of us, it just will not do. We identify with those who are willing to engage more positively with the new situation and who believe that it has much to offer to Christians, just as they have much to offer to it.

To some extent the separate approaches depend on how much people actually live in the world of the postmodern (or, as I would put it, the real world) rather than bumping into it and trying to avoid it. One of my friends said to me recently, 'I can see that a lot of positive changes are taking place in evangelicalism and I wish the people well. But the fact is, most of it has hardly anything at all to do with me or the world I live in.' Even more pointed are the words of the son of John V. Taylor, who when he decided to give up on the church apparently said to his father, 'Father, that man [the preacher] is saying all of the right things but he isn't saying them to anybody. He doesn't know where I am, and it would never occur to him to ask!'[1] As someone once said, 'Whenever I hear people saying "Christ is the answer", I always want to say, "Have you the remotest idea what the question is?" '

Let me summarize what I think are some of the key characteristics of this new postmodern world in which we live. It is a world in which people now reject truth claims which are expressed in the form of dogma or absolutes. It is a world in which dignity is granted to emotions and intuition, and where people are accustomed to communicating through words linked to images and symbols rather than through plain words or simple statements. It is a world in which people have come to feel a close affinity with the environment, and where there is a strong sense of global unity. It is a world in which people are deeply suspicious of institutions, bureaucracies and hierarchies. And perhaps most importantly of all, it is a world in which the spiritual dimension is once again talked about with great ease. Post-evangelical people, I think, are people who belong to, or are influenced by, this world, and whose Christian faith is increasingly being expressed in and through this frame of reference.

The fact that there is an upsurge of hunger for spirituality can be seen all around, and the selfish prosperity cult of the Thatcher and Reagan years has only added fuel to it. In her book *Stare Back and Smile*, the actress Joanna Lumley puts her finger on it: 'More spirituality and less materialism are what we need in the West . . . . In the 1990s we're going to start finding our souls again. We've gone through a very non-spiritual time this century.'[2] Our own daughter Jeni speaks of the palpable change of attitudes she detects among her peers: in the early 1980s they were very sceptical of anything to do with the spiritual realm, and talking about God was very difficult, whereas today people readily talk about spiritual things. Yet in most cases, people are not turning to the church to satisfy this hunger; instead, many are turning to some expression of the New Age. Christians often see this as a straightforward rejection of God in favour of satanic deceptions, but is it? John Drane does not see it this way; he states that the vast majority of New Agers are engaged in a serious search for God. 'If anything', he says, 'they are likely to be more open to a radical life-changing encounter with Christ than are many Christians.'[3]

So why is this? Why is it that in an age of almost unparalleled interest in spirituality, the church is still so incredibly unpopular. Even where churches are turning a corner and growing, the majority of this growth is still coming from church transfers. Let me just pinpoint three important points to be pondered.

The first is that the evangelical gospel tends to be much too 'refined'. In other words it is a systematized 'A–Z of Everything You Need to Know about Life, Death and Eternity' – it is a 'big story' approach to the Christian narrative. It is generally assumed that this 'package' represents New Testament Christianity, and yet nowhere was it presented in this way, either by Jesus or the apostles. The pre-packed gospel is really a systematized stringing together of lots of little pieces which in their original context were presented as they stood, without being fitted into a coherent scheme. For example, the young ruler asked what he might do to inherit eternal life: a question almost designed for a modern evangelistic response. Yet Jesus told him to keep the commandments and sell all that he had and give to the poor (Luke 18.19–22). Not a very well rounded gospel message! No mention of faith. No mention of salvation by grace and not works. No mention of 'making a prayer of commitment'!

We need to take seriously Brueggemann's idea of 'funding the postmodern imagination'. He says that when we offer a full alternative world to people, we are acting in the imperialistic style which postmodern people are actually rejecting. Rather than offering truth in the form of a dogmatic grand scheme, we must offer 'a lot of little pieces out of which people can put life together in fresh configurations.'[4]

In a similar vein, the usual approach to presenting the gospel assumes that 'We've got it – you need it!' But such dogmatic claims are unlikely to cut any ice in today's world. It is much more helpful to use the language of journey. It is quite wrong to think of the world as 'Christians over here on the right and non-Christians over there on the left', with evangelism understood as the task of shifting people from left to right. It is much more helpful to see that people are already on a spiritual journey, in which we can expect that God has been evidently present and at work, even if he is unrecognized by that name. And evangelism should no longer function as a kind of religious sales operation, which often depersonalizes the individual being evangelized, but instead be understood as an opportunity to 'fund' people's spiritual journey, drawing on the highly relevant resources of 'little pieces' of truth contained in the Christian narrative.

A recent survey of how people find faith showed that 69 per cent of people cannot put a date on their conversion: it was a gradual process – a journey. I believe I saw a Marc Europe leaflet which commented that twenty-five years ago, the statistic was exactly the opposite way round: 69 per cent said it was datable.[5] I am convinced that the cultural shift we have been discussing is a significant factor, if not the significant factor in this turn around. John Finney who conducted the recent survey (and it makes for very stimulating reading) says that those who evangelize often look for quick results, but in the light of this trend they should pause for thought. 'The gradual process is the way in which the majority of people discover God', he says, 'and the average time is about four years: models of evangelism which can help people along the pathway are needed.'[6] The concept of people being on a journey is apparently being borne out by the facts.

Corresponding to the notion of recognizing the validity of other people's journeyings towards God is a willingness to admit to the ups and downs of our own journey. When Bono of U2 said 'I still haven't found what I'm looking for', many evangelicals despaired, thinking that he had lost his way spiritually, but he was quite clear: 'You broke the bonds, you loosed the chains, you carried the cross and my shame. You know I believe it, but I still haven't found what I'm looking for.' This is not a statement of confusion, or spiritual ambivalence: quite the reverse, it is a positive recognition of the frailty of human experience and human comprehension. We all know only in part, we experience only in part, and in a postmodern world it is crucial that we are honest about this limitation.

The whole backdrop of the Christian gospel is the organized church and, sadly, this is the biggest stumbling block of all to the postmodern onlooker. 'The uncomfortable truth', John Drane says, 'is that the church has been all too eager to adopt the secular standards and practices of our prevailing Western culture.' The result of this is that people see in the church just more of what they see *and reject* in the outside world: hierarchies, bureaucracies, and power struggles. And as Drane says, 'They know that this is not what will bring them personal spiritual fulfilment.'[7] This is not a time for churches to be working towards 'bigger', 'better' and 'more powerful'; it is a time for the church to follow the example of its Lord and divest itself of its power, with all the personality jostling, political

manoeuverings and empire-building that goes with it –
the postmodern world is not impressed!

And Finally . . .

I said at the beginning of this book that I intended to
do three things: give a degree of explanation of what
was happening with regard to the emergence of the
post-evangelical, and why it is happening; give encouragement to those who were thinking and feeling in a
post-evangelical way, and wondering if they were
alone in doing so; and offer some alternative possibilities for those who are much clearer about where
they have come from than where they are going to. I
feel I have made a rather crude, but I hope honest,
attempt to deal with these three points. The subject-
matter covered is all rather basic, and begs many more
questions than it answers, but I think that this is the
way it should be. I would like to think that it will
stimulate the rigorous debate that is needed, as people
wrestle with the issues of living in a postmodern world,
and try to understand its full implications.

I can think of no better way to close than to quote
again the German ecologist Rudolph Bahro: 'When the
forms of an old culture are dying, the new culture is
created by a few people who are not afraid to be
insecure.'[8]

Notes

Chapter 1: A Symbol of Hope

1 William Abraham, *The Divine Inspiration of Holy Scripture* (Oxford: Oxford University Press, 1981), p. 113f.
2 Rowland Croucher, *Recent Trends Among Evangelicals* (NSW Australia: Albertross Books, 1986), p. 7.
3 John Drane, *What is the New Age Saying to the Church?* (London: Marshall Pickering, 1991).
4 John Drane, *New Age*, p. 203.

Chapter 2: We've Never Had it so Good!

1 Gerald Coates and Hugh Thompson, *Not Under Law* (London: Good Reading, 1975).
2 Ian Bradley, *Marching to the Promised Land* (London: John Murray, 1992), p. 55.
3 Bradley, *Marching*, p. 56.
4 Bradley, *Marching*, p. 57.
5 Graham Kendrick, Gerald Coates, Roger Forster, Lynn Green, *March for Jesus* (Eastbourne: Kingsway, 1992), pp. 153, 143.
6 Gerald Coates, 'Revival and the Status Quo', *Alpha*, October 1994.
7 Dave Roberts, 'Calver Speaks Out', *Alpha*, October 1994.
8 Gilles Kepel, *The Revenge of God* (Cambridge: Polity Press, 1994), pp. 1–12.

Chapter 3: Worlds Apart

1 Kwame Bediako, 'Biblical Christologies in the Context of African Traditional Religions', in Vinay Samuel and Chris Sugden (eds), *Sharing Jesus in the Two-Thirds World* (Michigan: Eerdmans, 1983), p. 83.

Notes

2 Bediako, 'Christologies', p. 89.
3 Tony Walter, *A Long Way From Home* (Exeter: Paternoster, 1979), p. 159.
4 Walter, *Long Way*, p. 160.
5 Anne Borrowdale, *Reconstructing Family Values* (London: SPCK, 1994), p. 68.
6 Quoted in Borrowdale, *Reconstructing*, p. 69.
7 Adrian Thatcher, *Liberating Sex: A Christian Sexual Theology* (London: SPCK, 1993), p. 84.
8 Walter, *Long Way*, p. 168.
9 George Marsden, *Fundamentalism and American Culture* (Oxford: Oxford University Press, 1980), p. 35.
10 C.S. Lewis, *The Four Loves* (Glasgow: Fount, 1960), p. 91f.
11 Tony Campolo interviewed in *21CC*, November 1990, p. 27.

Chapter 4: Longing to Grow

1 For example in James W. Fowler, *Stages of Faith: The Psychology of Human Development and the Quest for Meaning* (San Francisco: Harper and Row, 1982).
2 M. Scott Peck, *The Different Drum* (London: Arrow Books, 1990), ch. ix.
3 E. Berne, *Games People Play* (New York: Grove Press, 1964).
4 Thomas Harris, *I'm OK – You're OK* (London: Pan Books, 1973), p. 17.
5 John Barton, *People of the Book* (London: SPCK, 1988), p. 2.
6 Harry Blamires, *The Christian Mind* (London: SPCK, 1963), p. 50.

Chapter 5: Woolly Liberals?

1 Anthony Thiselton, *Two Horizons* (Exeter: Paternoster Press, 1980), p. 14f.
2 Colin Brown, *Philosophy and the Christian Faith* (London: IVP, 1973), p. 50f.
3 A good account of this period is given in Marsden, *Fundamentalism*, pt. 1.

4 Millard Erickson, *The New Evangelical Theology* (London: Marshall, Morgan and Scott, 1969), pp. 30–45.
5 *No More Mr Nice Guy* (Birmingham: SCM Publications, 1994).
6 John Saxbee, *Liberal Evangelism: A Flexible Response to the Decade* (London: SPCK, 1994), p. 19.
7 John Stratton Hawley, *Fundamentalism and Gender* (Oxford: Oxford University Press, 1994), p. 13f.
8 Walter Wink, *The Bible in Human Transformation* (Philadelphia: Fortress Press, 1973).
9 Walter Wink, *Transforming Bible Study* (London: Mowbray, 1990), ch. 1.

Chapter 6: 'Let Me Tell You a Story'
1 Graham Cray, based on 'From Here to Where – The Culture of the Nineties', unpublished paper, p. 5.
2 Angela McRobbie, 'Postmodernism and Popular Culture', in Lisa Appignanesi (ed.), *Postmodernism* (London: Free Association Books, 1989), p. 170.
3 McRobbie, 'Postmodernism', p. 168.
4 Gerard Loughlin, 'At the End of the World', in Andrew Walker (ed.) *Different Gospels* (London: SPCK, 1993), p. 208.
5 Hans Kung, *Global Responsibility* (London: SCM Press, 1990), pp. 2–6.
6 Zygmunt Bauman, *Postmodern Ethics* (Oxford: Blackwell, 1993), p. 32.
7 Walter Brueggemann, *The Bible and Postmodern Imagination* (London: SCM Press, 1993), p. 1.
8 Brueggemann, *The Bible*, p. 17.
9 Brueggemann, *The Bible*, p. 17.
10 Zygmunt Bauman, *Intimations of Postmodernity* (London: Routledge, 1993), p. *vii*f.
11 Bauman, *Intimations*, p. *x*f.
12 Bauman, *Ethics*, p. 33.
13 Drane, *New Age*, p. 203.
14 Drane, *New Age*, p. 239.
15 McRobbie, 'Postmodernism', p. 167.
16 Brueggemann, p. 20.
17 Rudolph Bahro, in Jonathan Porritt, *Seeing Green* (Oxford: Blackwell, 1984), frontispiece.

Chapter 7: The Truth, the Whole Truth and Something Quite Like the Truth

1 George Lindbeck, *The Nature of Doctrine* (London: SPCK, 1984), p. 8.
2 Ian Barbour, *Myths, Models and Paradigms* (San Francisco: Harper and Row, 1974), p. 105.
3 Vanhoozer, *Ricoeur's Philosophy and Hermeneutics* (Cambridge: Cambridge University Press, 1990), pp. 57–61.
4 Brueggemann, *The Bible*, p. 8.
5 Don Cupitt, *The Time Being* (London: SCM Press, 1992), p. 33.
6 Stephen Ross White, *Don Cupitt and the Future of Christian Doctrine* (London: SCM Press, 1994), p. 198f.
7 This idea is explained very clearly in Sallie McFague, *Models of God* (London: SCM Press, 1987), ch. 2.
8 E.J. Tinsley, 'Via Negativa' and 'Via Positiva', in *A New Dictionary of Christian Theology* (London: SCM Press, 1983), p. 596f.
9 James Richmond, 'Dialectical Theology', in *A New Dictionary*, p. 157f.
10 Janet Martin Soskice, *Metaphor and Religious Language* (Oxford: Clarendon Press, 1985), p. 160.
11 Ross White, *Don Cupitt*, pp. 206–9.
12 Ross White, *Don Cupitt*, p. 209f.
13 Brueggemann, *The Bible*, p. 10.
14 Barbour, *Myths*, pp. 179–81.

Chapter 8: Is the Bible the Word of God?

1 Francis Schaeffer, *The Great Evangelical Disaster* (Illinois: Crossway Books, 1984), p. 46f.
2 David Edwards, *Essentials: A Liberal–Evangelical Dialogue* (London: Hodder and Stoughton, 1988), p. 95.
3 Edwards, *Essentials*, pp. 49, 96f.
4 Edwards, *Essentials*, p. 101f.
5 James Barr, *Explorations in Theology 7* (London: SCM Press, 1980), p. 67.
6 Paul Achtemeier, *The Inspiration of Scripture: Problems and Proposals* (Philadelphia: Westminster Press, 1980), pp. 62–6.

7   Achtemeier, *Inspiration*, p. 67.
8   Achtemeier, *Inspiration*, p. 106.
9   Barr, *Explorations*, p. 70.
10 Karl Barth, *Against the Stream* (London: SCM Press, 1954), pp. 216–25.
11 Sandra Schneiders, *The Revelatory Text* (San Francisco: Harper and Collins, 1991), ch. 2.
12 Schneiders, *Revelatory*, p. 32f.
13 Schneiders, *Revelatory*, p. 35f.
14 Schneiders, *Revelatory*, p. 39.
15 Schneiders, *Revelatory*, p. 34f.
16 Quoted in Thomas Torrance, 'The Framework of Belief' in T. Torrance (ed.), *Belief in Science and in Christian Life* (Edinburgh: Handsel Press, 1980), p. 4.
17 Michael Polanyi, *Personal Knowledge* (New York: Harper and Row, 1964), p. 197.
18 Torrance, *Belief in Science and in Christian Life*, pp. 13–25.
19 Brueggemann, *The Bible*, p. 12f.
20 Wink, *Bible Study*.
21 Hans-Ruedi Weber, *Experiments with Bible Study* (Geneva: WCC Publications, 1989).

Chapter 9: Positively Worldly

1   From 'This World is Not My Home' in *Youth Praise* (London: Falcon for the Church Pastoral-Aid Society, 1968).
2   Charles Colton, *Lacon*, vol. 1, no. 408 (1820).
3   Jurgen Moltmann, *God in Creation: An Ecological Doctrine of Creation* (London: SCM Press, 1985), p. 29f.
4   Andrew Linzey, *Christianity and the Rights of Animals* (London: SPCK, 1987), pp. 36–7 and *passim*.
5   John Macquarrie, *Principles of Christian Theology* (London: SCM Press, 1966), p. 213.
6   Macquarrie, *Principles*, p. 61.
7   Macquarrie, *Principles*, p. 238.
8   Macquarrie, *Principles*, p. 245.
9   Michael Christensen, *C.S. Lewis on Scripture* (London: Hodder and Stoughton, 1979), p. 27.

10 M. Haralambos, *Sociology: Themes and Perspectives* (London: Bell and Hyman, 1986), p. 3.
11 Haralambos, *Sociology*, p. 3f.
12 Donald Miller, *The Case for Liberal Christianity* (London: SCM Press, 1981), p. 34.
13 Michel Quoist, *Prayers of Life* (Dublin: Gill and Macmillan, 1963).

Chapter 10: Christianity for a New Age

 1 Graham Cray, 'From Here to Where: The Culture of the Nineties', unpublished paper, p. 13.
 2 Drane, *New Age*, p. 15.
 3 Drane, *New Age*, p. 213.
 4 Brueggemann, *The Bible*, p. 20.
 5 *Land Marc*, Spring 1993 (London: Marc Europe, 1993).
 6 John Finney, *Finding Faith Today: How does it Happen?* (Swindon: BFBC, 1992), p. 24f.
 7 Drane, *New Age*, p. 236.
 8 Porritt, *Seeing Green*, frontispiece.